LIZ KAVANAGH
FROM THE HORSE'S MOUTH

WOLFHOUND PRESS
Celebrating 25 Years

First published in 1999 by
Wolfhound Press Ltd
68 Mountjoy Square
Dublin 1, Ireland
Tel: (353-1) 874 0354
Fax: (353-1) 872 0207

British Library Cataloguing in Publication Data
A catalogue record for this book is available from the British Library.

ISBN 0-86327-750-0

10 9 8 7 6 5 4 3 2 1

Cover Photograph: G.A. Duncan
Cover Design: Slick Fish Design
Typesetting: Wolfhound Press
Printed in the Republic of Ireland by Colour Books, Dublin.

Contents

INTRODUCTION

When looking for a title for this collection I asked the family for suggestions. Quick as a flash came the riposte from one son 'there's only one possible name this time, Mom — *The Thorn In Our Sides*'. So there and then, on the spot, I determined that, come what may, none of them was going to see the finished work beforehand. Despite this dig I cannot change what I am — a compulsive discloser — hence *The Horse's Mouth*.

Yes, I do get into trouble for what I write. I now fully understand, why, almost a quarter of a century ago, when I first started to write, I never told a single soul, not even my five sons about it. That was a marvellous freedom back then, when neither family nor neighbours knew. But now the sons all have wives, hence double trouble, and everybody else knows as well, yet I still just must continue to write. It is an addiction. I have no choice really.

How Eoin 'puts up with the whole country knowing all about his private affairs' is the real mystery to everyone. I never, ever, show him the article before I send it off. If I had to, I'd lose my courage on the spot. As a matter of fact I don't even like being in the same room as him when I see him coming to my part of the *Farmers' Journal*. Eoin meticulously starts at the beginning and works steadily through the whole publication. So, when I see him picking up the *Journal* I have time enough to beat a hasty retreat. And, all going well, he will have forgotten what I have written, after he has perused each and every one of the small ads. Life continues to run smoothly just so long as I'm not there at the time of reading.

I just hate it, however, when he brings the *Journal* to bed with him to read. That limits my options severely. A rush call to the loo cannot delay me sufficiently long enough, I've discovered. I have also been known to take a sudden notion, late and all that it might be, that a long hot soak in the bath would be just the thing for my aching back. That works fine unless I've already have had a bath before going to bed. Then, even my poor innocent would smell some kind of a rat.

On such nights I am forced to resort to distraction therapy, to get Eoin's mind off his *Journal* and on to other matters. He can't read the *Journal* with the lights out after all. However, at our age, such tactics don't always work. So, what I really need right now is a supply of certain lozenge-shaped blue-coloured pills for his use. If those are all they are cracked up to be, Eoin reading the *Journal* in bed beside me will be the least part of my worries. And, even if they are not, sure we can still have fun trying. Since writers are compulsive disclosers, doubtless I'll let you know the result if and when the time comes that Eoin is tempted, or persuaded, to look for a prescription for that five-letter product which begins with a V. I do have the right, after all, to write of my own experiences, whatever about those of others.

JANUARY

New Year Customs (1997)

When does the new year start for you? That probably seems a stupid enough question. The tax year and milk quota year, of course, starts in April. Here, our calving year starts in October. And I believe that you can choose whenever you like to start your financial year.

The New Year customs, however, have always been tied up with 1 January. Yet a neighbour said to me during the week, talking of the changes here, each son going their separate way and Eoin and myself taking a back seat, that, since there wasn't a new moon at the New Year, he did not think it was such a good idea for us to be in too much of a rush, but to wait for the January new moon to finalise anything. Then, and only then, or so he said, was the proper time to make changes, or even one's New Year resolutions. And it was foolish to otherwise tempt providence.

'You can't go against nature and the natural rhythms' he said. This was a totally new one on me, and I thought I had heard all the customs and superstitions about both the new moon, Christmas and the New Year. I know a new moon at any time of the year is lucky, once you don't see it through glass. And, to make sure of your luck for the coming lunar month, you really should, on first sight, turn over the money in your pocket, blessing yourself and saying a prayer for all the dear departed at the same time.

This is especially the case when the new moon happily co-incides with the New Year. Then, by doing all that, you could be really sure of a very prosperous twelve months, or thirteen lunar months, to come. But I never knew that you could, by adopting this man's logic, increase your chances of a good year by deciding that the new moon was really the beginning of the New Year and not just the January First date on the calendar.

Still and all, for me, the mark of each new year beginning is the cock's step of lengthening daylight, which really does start after the first of January, regardless of when the new moon falls. I watch for that cock's step and always comment on it because that is the beginning of life again. I swear I noticed it yesterday evening, and felt good as a result.

Talking of cocks, if the cock crowed at midnight on New Year's Eve, in conjunction with the new moon, that was the best sign possible of the year to come for that household. There's hardly a hen-cock left in the country now, except the few seemingly kept to annoy the neighbours. However, when such a belief was widespread, which isn't that long ago either, the New Year was welcomed in, at midnight, by the ringing of church bells, and the parading of young men from village to village with every possible noise making instrument they could lay their hands on. So, could anything be more calculated to set all the cocks of the country crowing? Now, the young men no longer leave the pubs to frighten away the demons of the winter, and, with their noise and vigour, help Spring to come in. The noise and commotion on New Year's Eve, is now confined to the cities and towns and has nothing to do with the fear of an agricultural people that perhaps Spring would not return, unless it was welcomed and encouraged to do so by noise and merriment at the turn of the year.

Whatever about us supposed to be taking a back seat Eoin and I welcomed in the New Year with the birth of a calf at precisely midnight and it was a few minutes into the new year when we thought to check our watches. The young people were out, as it is only fitting for the young to welcome in the New Year with a little more ceremony than jacking a calf, when they have still got somebody at home to look after things. Actually it was Eoin was asked to keep an eye on both of our son's places and I was only called out when he failed to get a giddy cow to stay still enough to be delivered of her calf.

I was baby-sitting my granddaughters but they were sound asleep at this stage. My bedtime stories were not fairy stories that night. Instead, when we had that flurry of snow, I told them that it was the way the angels were plucking a goose to make New Year's Day dinner for God in Heaven and how there would be still one goose left for the Women's Christmas next week. I found myself telling them how water is supposed to be turned to wine at midnight, rushes to silk, and gravel to gold, on the eve of that, the very last night of Christmas. Michaella just loves all my stories.

She looked at me, blue eyes shining, all excitement, as I tried to remember times past, and more of the stories I had been told. I was half expecting the next question to be why God couldn't make His own dinner. But, instead, she flummoxed me by asking me what was Heaven and who was God. So I had to explain more than I bargained for. Still and all she has another two years to go to her First Communion. My only worry is now is if I have her hopelessly confused.

I already had told her how I will keep one piece of holly to cook the first pancake on Shrove Tuesday night. She, there and then, got out of bed to help me put a piece of holly up beside the piece of blessed palm we brought home from Mass last Palm Sunday and stuck, as usual, on top of the picture of the Sacred Heart. So, imagine my predicament explaining such a strange mixture of paganism and Christianity to a six-year-old child. Explaining why Jesus had his heart, in the picture, showing on the outside wasn't that easy either.

Then it struck me that when we, in Ireland, tell of our old customs, we presume a basic grounding in the tenets of Christianity. I had already told Michaella of the animals being able to talk at midnight on Christmas Eve night in honour of the Holy Family wandering the earth in search of a lodging place. I was reminded of this story as I moved our New Year's candle to the window in the hall so that its light could shine out. She told me that her Mummy only had a Christmas candle, not a New Year's one, but they never lit it this year.

I suppose there aren't that many of us left with our three big red candles on the Christmas shopping list every year. Customs change as the generations pass. It probably took

many generations to change pagan rites to Christianity and now
God knows where the changes are going with the new generation. The eternal rhythms, however, do not change. The daylight
still lengthens, by a cock's step every day, from New Year's day
onwards, regardless of what people do.

At my age I can see how all the customs that once marked
out our hours also marked the time passing for us. Pure super-
stition they mostly were, of course, but these superstitions did
give a structure to life and I am inclined to miss them and also
to cling to them since I do believe that any or all such things
enrich rather than impoverish life. And my grandchildren love
the telling. My big mistake that night, when I was asked who
God is, was that I didn't tell her to ask her father next day when
she went home. If he had a sore head after his celebrations of
the night before that would indeed test him out. And serve him
right, too.

Happy New Year everybody.

Oh What a Night it Was? (1978)

I'm still laughing to myself about Friday night. And now that
Eoin's head is better he is able to join me in the laughter. It
surely was a cocktail party we'll remember.

We hadn't been to a cocktail party for years, or drinks party,
as they now seem to be called. These are one of Eoin's pet hates.
He just hates being jam-packed into a room with a crowd of
strangers. As he himself cheerfully admits he is no good at
talking about nothing. Unless he meets up with a fellow farmer,
or an old friend, he always seems to end up with his back
against a wall and an empty glass in his hand: he is no good
either at helping himself to drinks. As a result, we have, for years,
declined any such invitations as came our way. Eoin says anyway that they are a cheapskate way of returning our hospitality.

I did not accept this time either: I just didn't answer in time.
'Drinks 6.30 to 8pm ... regrets only' ran the invitation. As is my
usual custom I stuck it on the dresser in the kitchen when it
came and there it languished among the unpaid bills. Except

that the nights are still dark and Eoin was in early from the cows I don't think I'd ever have persuaded him to go.

As it was he said that he didn't have time for his tea — it wouldn't be worth while going at all if he stopped to eat now he said. 'They'll surely have sausages and stuff there anyway, so I'll fill up on those...,' he threw over his shoulder at me as he raced upstairs to wash. I suppose, seeing me all dressed up, he hadn't the heart to disappoint me. I do dearly love an outing of any sort where I've a chance to meet up with interesting people. So Eoin went off on an empty stomach: I had had my tea earlier with the boys.

The party was as expected — too many people crowded together in a room, all talking together at the tops of their voices with nobody at all listening. The noise came out the front door to meet us. And standing just inside the door was a white-coated barman behind a table groaning with bottles.

'Tell Tom what you're drinking and he'll see after you both then for the rest of the night,' said our host to Eoin as he took me into the packed room, splitting up an established group to fit me in.

'This is Liz Kavanagh — a farmer's wife,' was my introduction, with no names at all for the strange faces taking me in.

'Oh really!' was the languid reaction. 'I must say you don't look in the least like a farmer's wife — much too glamorous...'

I felt my hackles rise on the spot, but still managed to make small talk as Tom, the barman, pressed a vodka and white into my hand. I know that remark was meant as a compliment, but comments like that always infuriate me. What did they expect me to look like, I wonder? With a sack apron and the mark of the Wellingtons still on my red legs I suppose?

The chit-chat went on in this vein, the benefits of the easy country life, being close to nature and all that. I played along all right, talking about the satisfaction in feeding calves, and how pronounced the suckling instinct is in all young things. Then, this well-endowed woman in a low-cut little black number bent towards me.

'How interesting...,' she said. 'But do tell me my dear. Do hens suckle their young? It's something I've always wanted to know.'

How I didn't choke on my drink is something I'll never know. But I was spared an explanation because at that very moment my host took me by the arm to join another group. He was a very good host that way. I will be forever more, however, haunted by visions of that poor woman, still going around, asking any farmer she meets, if hens suckle their young. I spoke to her no more that night with the press of people.

Eventually I spotted Eoin, not with his back to a wall, but seemingly fascinated by a woman holding forth in his group. His glass wasn't empty either and, while I watched, Tom topped it up once more. So there and then I decided to put my hand over my glass when next Tom came my way. Having a barman meant that this party was no cheap lift, I reckoned. People weren't in the least loth to ask him to freshen their drinks when some would be slow to ask their host or hostess to do so.

Finally, I joined up with Eoin, briefly, to find out how he was doing and what was so fascinating about that woman earlier on. Eoin was happy out and I quickly discovered the cause of his fascination.

'She fascinated me Liz because she never, not even for a moment, stopped talking. I've no idea really what she was going on about, but I found myself drawing breath for her...'

I dare say she felt that if she wasn't talking she wasn't being a success at the party. I felt a little bit that way myself as I initiated conversations with utter and total strangers. My host was no longer leading me around. I think he thought that, being a farmer's wife, I mightn't be able to cope. Tom, with his circulating bottles, however, was wonderful for loosening all tongues. And anyway, I already knew that to be silent at this kind of a party is the ultimate social sin. Quantity and not quality has to be the order of the day.

It was Eoin, however, who heard what I thought was the prize snippet of the night, if you exclude my woman. While leaning, momentarily, against a wall two acquaintances met up beside him.

'My dear — I have such good news to tell you,' said one.

'Do tell,' came the breathless reply.

'Well,' continued the first, 'I was down to the glass-houses

today to see my little lettuces and they are already so high...'
indicating with finger and thumb.

'Oh my dear,' gushed the other. 'I'm so-o happy for you...'

It was hours later that I heard all about the little lettuces, in
the car, going home. When eight o'clock came and there obviously wasn't going to be any food served, I went in search of
Eoin, to go home. I could see that people were starting to drift
away and no way did I want to be the last to leave. Eoin, however, when I discovered him, was in the pristine kitchen, quite
happy with a group of men and half-filled bottles, busily set-
tling the affairs of the nation.

Two hours later the die-hards were still hard at it but I'd had
more than enough. So I prised Eoin out of the still unfinished
business of the nation by telling him that maybe there were
cows calving at home. I then decided that I'd better do the
driving even though he was fully lucid, telling me all about the
little lettuces.

Anyway, I dropped him off at the maternity unit, for one
quick check of the cows, while I went around to the front of the
house with the car and then into the kitchen to put down a fine
feed of rashers and eggs. I felt we both needed them — badly. I
even fried up some cold potatoes, to soak up the bacon fat —
and the alcohol. Then I realised that Eoin should have been in
long ago, no matter what was happening, since he was only in
his good suit and shoes.

I went looking for him, reluctantly donning my wellingtons
and work-wear, with the smell of the fry-up strong in my nos-
trils. It must have been something really seriously wrong when
he hadn't first come in to change. In the maternity ward there
was a cow in the calving pen all right, and she was also freshly
calved even though I couldn't see the calf she was busily licking
on her upper side. There was no trace of Eoin however. Crossly,
I decided the wretch must be over in the waiting ward, despite
wearing his good clothes. So I went into the cow to check the
sex of the calf for the records.

I never got around to that, however. The poor cow was disturbed enough without me making the story worse. She had a
calf all right, just freshly born, too, as I had thought. But the
poor cow was in an awful quandary. She didn't quite know

which to lick, her calf, or Eoin, who was lying stretched out beside it and the cleaning, oblivious to everything, with the calving jack still beside him. He had obviously calved the cow safely, and then collapsed, out for the count. I laughed and laughed looking at him and his foster-mother.

Then I managed, somehow, to pull him to his feet and into the house. But I regret one thing very deeply — that I didn't leave him where he was and run in home for the camera first — and to hell with the damage he was doing to his good suit.

What Do Bank Managers Know Anyway? (1986)

Well, how do you personally feel about bank managers and farming? We had to go and see ours this week — a royal summons. And, since he was only appointed some months ago, it was our first time meeting him across his desk. We do so hate changes in bank managers — probably a case of 'the devil you know....' Yet, over the years, the change always proved to be for the best — once we had the new man broken in.

It was far from that situation when we were first married, however. That manager, or Agent as they were then called in the Bank of Ireland, was never, ever, at his desk when Eoin was ushered into his presence. Always he stood, apparently unaware of Eoin's existence, looking out the window onto the street, filling his pipe with infinite care. Eoin was left standing, for what seemed like endless ages, at the far side of his desk. He never knew whether he was expected to say hello to that silent implacable back, sit down on the one chair placed in readiness, or cough to get attention.

Eoin, being who he is, just stood there, silently, feeling smaller and smaller, and less and less sure of how he was going to explain the overdrawn state of his bank account this time. Mr Thompson was never any help as he continued to survey the passing traffic in silence and fiddle with his pipe, which, incidentally, Eoin never once saw him light. It was always left, shamelessly cold, on the ashtray, once it had served its purpose.

On coming out again, Eoin used to call him all sorts of

names. His use of the pipe especially infuriated him. Eoin was certain that, on his departure, the thing was just emptied back into the agent's tobacco pouch, ready to start the same perform-ance all over again with the next poor unfortunate waiting in line outside. One never, ever, got called in at the appointed time., Always the customer had to wait.

Now we know that Mr Thompson was a past master at secur-ing for himself the dominant role in interviews with clients. That was what the whole charade was all about, of course, the silence, the waiting, and the big imposing desk and his chair so very much bigger and better than that in readiness for the interviewee. And all this worked. Eoin absolutely hated being summoned to his office. Those little white envelopes coming in the post, with the information that he was to be in the Agent's office on such a day and such a time, destroyed his nights' sleep and his days' ease until it was all over until the next time.

I, myself, never met the man. In the fifties, wives just did not go along as well. It wasn't the done thing, man's work and all that. So, it was always men only in the waiting line. In fact, I used to stay in the car outside, to await our fate, even though I was the one who had, invariably, made out the stock inventory and/or the cash-flow projections for Eoin to explain. Eoin always said that Mr Thompson knew nothing whatsoever about farming and he had to explain everything in the simple detail he could understand.

Then, there were none of those friendly, father-figure bankers that the advertisements would have you believe are in every branch these days. And Eoin had reason for believing bankers knew nothing about farming having been forced into some very stupid decisions early on in his farming career. I must have heard a million times, how, to bring down his overdraft, he was forced, one year, into selling his spring hoggets before they were fit at all. The price was very bad as a result, and he also finished up having to plough in tremendous fields of grass simply because he had nothing to eat it. Immediate overdraft reduction was more important to that Agent than sure eventual profits. That lack of elementary farming knowledge formed the basis of Eoin's complaints about him and some subsequent bank man-agers. As he put it they knew sweet all about farming yet they acted so superior in themselves.

Times changed, however, and the bankers changed too. Now, it is always a case of the outstretched hand at the office door and then a chair pulled out for me to sit on. You see I always go with Eoin now, and he often laughingly says that that's how he, in his turn, wrong-footed those gentlemen. They have to be polite to a woman. Tricks like turning their backs on a lady would only demean themselves and not me. Terribly complicated, isn't it, this psychological warfare in business? It is vitally important, however, to appear self-confident regardless of the somersaults butterflies may be turning in one's stomach.

Bank managers, and I do have this straight from the horse's mouth, tend to be favourably disposed to farmers who bring their wives along as well. Their statistics show that it is the farmers, who have wives actively involved in the business of farming, who tend to be the more successful. Men, it appears, have the happy knack of ignoring unpalatable facts in the hope that they might go away of their own accord. They can run away from their problems by borrowing, perhaps, from several sources and never once adding up the grand total.

Money owing to the hire-purchase companies becomes something that they do not have to worry about right now since it will mostly be paid out of the incomes of years to come. Even the harvest account at the Co-op, at this time of the year, is not something that should give them cause for concern. Next harvest is far away in the distance and maybe, after a really bumper harvest, things will be better by then. That, however, is something that cannot be relied on in this climate of ours as we well know to our cost.

So that is why I think that some form of a suitable business course should almost be mandatory for farmers' wives, because, even with the best skill as well as the will, the men just will not do their book-work when they come in, dog-tired, each night. And the notion that it is somehow not feminine to be able to add two and two together went out with the hooped skirt and the crinoline even though I fear that there may be still vestiges of such a way of thinking still around.

Only this week, at the country market, when some of us were bemoaning that last interest rate hike, one farmer's wife asked us what difference would it really make to any of us anyway. I, flippantly, said that she'd see the difference soon enough when she got this month's bank statement next month, and she would also see it later this month when the Co-op. increased their harvest account interest rate to match.

She just looked at me, with those big blue eyes, and said that both of those came addressed to John, so, of course, she never looked at them. I wonder if the said John was getting love letters through the post would she open those? Not that there has been the least whisper of anything like that doing the rounds, I hasten to add. But John really should buy his wife a letter opener and a calculator, as a late Christmas present, if there is any basis to the rumours going the rounds about the state of his financial affairs.

But will you just listen to me pontificating away as usual. I'm afraid I tended to be a little like that too with our new bank manager. He seemed a pleasant, approachable sort of an individual. So, our immediate business attended to, I asked him straight out what he knew about farming now that he had been moved from the city out here. I capped this by telling him our opinion of the general level of bank manager's knowledge on that subject.

He, however, took the wind completely out of my sails by agreeing with me. Then he went on to ask Eoin if it would be all right if some day soon he was to bring out his staff, after closing time, for a farm walk on our place to educate them from the very basics up. What could Eoin do but say yes — and I couldn't resist adding that it was all right by me too...

The Desolation of Ordinary Living (1997)

On my travels during the week, I met a woman, who, when I introduced myself, said:

'Ah yes, Liz Kavanagh, you are the woman who, as my husband says, writes so well about the desolation of ordinary living.'

That phrase, the desolation of ordinary living, stuck in my mind because it was so eloquently descriptive of frequent periods of farming life here. And, I was then told in detail, how it was such a relief to them, to regularly read of all the things that go wrong on our farm. They found it a help to hear of somebody else also suffering the stresses and strains of farming life, since most articles written for farmers, by men, just tell success stories, or else ways to farm still better and more profitably.

Stress and strain is mighty hard to avoid here, this time of the year especially, with quota problems, cows calving, beef animals for sale with bad prices and grading problems, and our accountant putting on the pressure so that he can finalise our tax accounts and have them in by the end of the month. And, as he reminded us, since we are on the averaging system it will take three years for this year's drop in income to work its way through the system so we are not to expect any great tax refunds this year. So, we are stressed wondering just who we are working for.

But really stress is a subject that is hard to avoid at any time of the year. These days you can't pick up a magazine or newspaper without articles on stress and ways of coping with same. And there is a whole plethora of books on occupational stress. Yet, how come we never heard of the word when I was growing up? Then one could be killed with work all right, but never with stress. Farmers then never suffered stress: they suffered want, hardship and poverty instead. So, the question I would like answered is can you suffer from something before you know it exists?

I was in the chemist's during the week. And, as I was waiting my turn, my eyes idly wandered along the shelves, looking at nothing in particular. However, my attention fixed on a whole row of patent medicines to relieve stress. There were pink bottles and blue cartons, white pills and red liquid. In fact, you name it and it was there. There were even handouts telling how stress is a fact of all our busy modern-day lives and how we should watch for the danger signs of stress. If we then answer yes to a certain number of questions, we should go pop a pill, or words to that effect.

And what was out on the shelves was probably nothing in comparison to what was behind the dispensing counter, the anti-depressant pills, the anti-anxiety pills, stacks of prescription 'happy' pills, etc. So somebody, somewhere, is making money out of us all being stressed out of our minds. All that started me thinking about precisely which set of people were buying such stuff in a small rural town like that. The row of contraceptives on the counter top, had also briefly caught my eye: somebody must be buying those as well or else they wouldn't be there.

The interesting thing about all this emphasis on stress is the blurring of the boundary between stress and distress. All the books, articles in magazines and the pills in the chemists' seem to say that the stresses we feel in our everyday lives are up to ourselves to cure, by changing our life style, or taking a pill, or going to a doctor, when we find ourselves stressed by our inability to meet various expectations or demands. Then everything will be fine.

But it is by no means as simple as that, as the suicide rates for farmers, recently released by the Minister of Health, so frighteningly revealed. There is no point in telling the person already over quota, three-quarters way only through the quota year, because of his normal expectation of temporary leasing, or the cattle farmer bedevilled by BSE, to go pop a pill. That will do nothing for harsh economic reality, whatever about the profits of the pharmaceutical companies.

And I have no answers either, beyond saying that I am glad that I am not young any more and that the main weight now falls on the shoulders of our young people. But I'll tell you this much. If it wasn't for them I'd be strongly tempted to get out altogether from farming by leasing the land and quota to other poor devils.

One couple I know of, in their sixties, whose children have all left and are not coming back farming, did just that. They got forty five pence a gallon for their quota and one hundred and fifty pounds an acre for each acre they rented with it: they did not rent the yard. So it is now a silent farmyard, the milking machine units are all hanging up and gathering dust, just as they were left the last time cows were milked there.

The interesting thing about all this, as one neighbour remarked, is that both husband and wife already look ten years younger and are quite calm and relaxed in themselves. However, he added, the man who rented their land and quota already looks

twenty years older, thus making up for their ten years apiece.
And no wonder too, since he is now landed with costs of 60p a
gallon on that quota, before he feeds a pound of meal to the
cows, or uses a unit of electricity.

But then again, as a thought for the week, we work not only
to produce but to give value to time. This Summer that retired
couple relaxed and enjoyed life. But what reason will they have
to get up in the mornings from now on...

FEBRUARY

A Little Case of DIY (1991)

Well, I'll have to get stuck into a marathon bake by this weekend because at long last her parents have got around to organising a date for my granddaughter's christening. It is to be next Saturday. And they only just told us that they had gone to the parish priest last night to fix up the day and the time. They also told us that they were inviting all and sundry. Eoin gave a big sigh of relief. I can only hope they didn't notice it with me jumping in to say I'd do some baking and what should I make for them. I wouldn't mind but I am killed telling Eoin these past weeks to say nothing to them, that it's their own affair when they have the child baptised and it's nothing whatsoever to do with us. Times are very different now to when our children were born, I kept telling him, and really we should consider ourselves fortunate that they are having her christened at all.

A frightening number of babies are not being baptised at all by young parents who have given up the complete practice of their religion, be they single mothers or couples with, or without, their marriage licences. Now those I've heard about are all city based, where I suppose nobody knows, and cares less, what any of their neighbours are doing. It is still different, however, in the country.

I have been asked, and on more than the one occasion too, if the child is christened yet? And, when I say no, they hasten to assure me that my son and daughter-in-law are dead right since there is no point in taking a baby out in bad weather and that the mother must get really strong again, poor thing. I know

quite well that they are only priming the pump to see if I will
say any more on the subject. Post-natal depression, or the like, is
the only reason those of my generation, or older, can see for not
having a child christened long before it is six weeks old. They,
after all, were, like me, brought up in the old school, in fear of
the consequences of our every action, deed or omission — I
forget the exact words of the catechism but not their meaning.
To miss Mass without good cause was to risk an eternity in hell
if we were to die before our next confession. But not to have a
baby baptised, a baby that could die at any minute, was an even
worse sin because then not only would we be damned for our
sin of omission but the poor innocent baby would, because of
that, be condemned to an eternity in a place called Limbo, never
to see the face of God. All the Masses and indulgences going
could not take an unbaptised baby out of Limbo the way they
could get a soul out of purgatory. So we were well warned
never to have that on our consciences. We learned exactly how
to baptise a child in an emergency and even about baptism by
desire.

Indeed a grandmother I know very well indeed, whose
grandchildren are of an English mother and living in England,
took the matter into her own hands last summer when the
second child arrived on the scene. It was only then that she
discovered that the eldest child had never been baptised when
her son said that they had no notion of going through all that
mumbo-jumbo with the new baby either. My friend must have
asked him the direct question because no way could I see him
volunteering that sort of information in cold blood over the
phone. He was always the type of lad who would do anything
for a quiet life, just like his father before him.

Up to this it was a particular grievance of the grandmother
that she had not been invited to her first grandchild's baptism.
I know because I heard all about it often enough God knows. I
was also told of her plans when she, immediately after that phone
call, went and booked a flight for herself to London. She even
showed me the lemonade bottle of holy water she was taking
with her in her bag, 'to do the job properly', as she said since
she intended, at the very first opportunity she got, to hold her
own very private baptism ceremony for her two grandchildren.

She'd have no bother, of course, with the new baby. He'd have no idea at all what was going on when she poured the holy water on his little head. But I did wonder what the three year old would make of it all, or how she'd report back on it to her parents. Children of that age would hang you, you know. So I eagerly awaited the next instalment of the story on my friend's return.

It appears, however, that everything went very smoothly indeed. The very first time she was left alone with the children Granny produced a brand new doll and then made a little game out of first baptising the doll with the name of Miranda, then the baby, Ralph, and finally, Emma, the little three year old, who thought the whole thing such great fun that she insisted that the family dog, Prince, be christened with holy water as well.

'And did you?' I asked, seeing nothing more profane about using holy water on a dog than a doll. That I had seen done before anyway.

I once had come upon my sons as they said 'I baptise thee, Kieran, in the name of the Father and of the Son and of the Holy Ghost. Amen,' as they generously poured the bottle of Easter water they had obviously swiped from the hall press, on the head of one of the two little pups we had allowed them to keep out of a litter. The other pup was already baptised John, I was told. Why all of this I have no idea unless they had been learning about John the Baptist in school and that baptism in the Jordan gave them the notion. They were so attached to those little pups, little dotes, a cross between our red setter and a visiting Labrador, that they wanted them to have the right start in life.

Unfortunately it didn't work, however, unless there is a Limbo for dogs, because less than a month later those two pups went missing one day. All day the boys searched high and low for them, not even stopping for meals. That night they were found, floating, in the slurry pit. And it all happened so simply too. A load of manure had been temporarily dumped in the yard, out of the way, up against the wall of the slurry pit. It, of course, months later, had made a perfect run-up for John and Kieran to climb to their death. Bitter tears were shed that night. Still we held a really grand funeral service for them, at dusk, over in the orchard, using up the last of the Easter holy water in the process. Fresh flowers were put on their graves every day, for about a week, until the novelty wore off and they forgot. John and Kieran may not have died in vain, however, because that heap of manure was quickly shifted and I can assure you we never made that mistake again. It could so easily have been a child that time and not the dogs.

I know all that is quite a number of years ago now. But thinking about it reminds me that before Michaella starts walking I must do a survey of all the potential death traps, in both farm and garden, and take suitable remedial action. Quite a lot of the protective fencing we put up when our own children were small is long gone, demolished by time as well as machinery. At the time we put chain-link fencing on seven foot high concrete posts, bent outwards, around the slurry pits. However, continued tips with silage tractors eventually brought most of the posts toppling down. Then the chain-link fencing got entangled in his silage trailer by a careless operator. This completed the demolition.

All that must be properly replaced, this time around, with great rockers of stones or even iron bars sunk in the ground to deter the taking of unnecessary short cuts. Anyway, we'll have a year or two to think up some suitable plan before Missy Michaella starts exploring on her own. And who knows? She may even grow up to be a real lady-like little girl never straying far from home. We shall have to wait and see just as we shall have to wait as see who are to be the godparents. In our relief that a date had been set for her christening we forgot to ask her parents that important question today. Evidently it isn't going to be either of us or we would have been asked on the spot.

I later confessed to Eoin that I'd had the faintest of faint hopes that I might have been asked to be the godmother. But I didn't confess that he needn't have been so worried about his little granddaughter not being baptised because I had done that job, weeks ago, with the Christmas holy water.

A Present from Charlie Haughey (1993)

'Is he still alive? Good God I thought he was dead long ago! — that's what they will be saying about me next—' said Eoin when the teasing started, and he was only half joking, you know. That is exactly what you do hear people saying when anybody goes beyond a certain age and are not seen out and about much anymore. But nobody could dream of saying that about Eoin for simply ages yet.

It's that time of the year again, however. His birthday is looming. And once again he doesn't want to know. It makes him feel old just to think about it, he says. And we hear of all the relations who were dead long before they got to his age. And there is no point in asking him what he'd like for a present. He always says that there is nothing he really needs despite our saying that presents can, and indeed should, be pure luxuries, especially at our time of life.

There is extra teasing going on at the moment, because normally nobody dares tease him too much coming up to his birthday. This teasing is because he is due a present from the government this year, the right to the free travel. All he has to do now is to apply for it, but he does not appear at all anxious to go about it. I really can't understand why he keeps putting off even getting the photographs taken. I had sent away for the forms long ago, because he would have kept putting that on the long finger as well. I know that if it was my case, I'd be all ready on the day. Anything going for nothing and I am always all for it anyway. You should see me in the supermarket going from free tasting to free tasting of food and then washing the whole lot down with several of those little phials of wine when I don't even like the taste of the stuff. But when anything is going for nothing, I am the first in the queue, regardless.

I do think that Eoin should be in there in the queue for his free travel if only because it will then mean that I can travel free too, just so long as I am with Eoin. I have visions of us just heading off into the wide blue yonder so to speak, or at least heading off to all the places in Ireland we've never been. I can see the two of us in lovely fine weather just taking the notion and heading off on a whim to the far reaches of Donegal or the remote resorts of Cork and Kerry. There we could stay in a nice hotel or guesthouse for a few days perhaps, until we grew tired of it, and then we could hop on the nearest bus or train and go on a sort of a mystery tour, because when we were not paying it really would not matter where we went. There is only one thing wrong with that lovely dream — Eoin does not qualify for the pension as well as the free travel and staying in hotels or even guesthouses can be far from cheap. He was just the wrong age when the compulsory PRSI payments came in for farmers. So he has paid up all those years since but not a tosser will he ever see out of it, it seems. I know that he can apply to have some of those moneys returned but we have been advised that while there is any hope of getting a pro-rata pension for his years contributing, that we would be advised to let things stand as they are. Once he takes back the money no matter what change of heart the government have, his right to even a small pension might then be gone. But to be realistic about it I suppose a snowball in hell has the same chance as Eoin has, of ever seeing anything back for his money.

We did contribute too, over the years, to the farmers' pension scheme with the FBD, but with things on the financial front the way they are, Eoin's pension there is nothing like we had expected from the salesman's spiel all those years ago. It was even worth more when he was first able to cash it in than it is now. And at that time we decided to wait for a few years for it to grow more, to give us that bit more security for the rest of our days. And our tongues weren't hanging out for it either to be quite truthful about the situation. And now we are waiting for the property markets or unit trusts or what ever it is, to recover. And all the time the years of good money actually in our fist are slipping away. So I keep telling Eoin that he is going to have to live a long, long time now to get his money's worth out of his pension fund.

And I'll tell you this much, as soon as my pensions come due I am going to take the money and run. And with me fortunately it is going to be pensions, because the state will be due to pay up a pension to me because I was well on the right side of fifty five when our PRSI payments started, and I also have a farmers pension in my own name. I am now getting old enough to find that fact a great comfort. To have your own money in your own hand to do what you like with, every week of the year must be a marvellous feeling especially for farm women. The money that comes in here for cattle, the monthly milk cheque, or whatever, these are regularly spent before they ever get here, or are ear-marked for something very important like reducing bank over-drafts. And it is always a long and uncertain wait for the next cheque. But to be able to go to the local post office every week of the year and put your hand out for the money, well now that must be a fine thing indeed at the end of your days, especially if you are not dependant on it. That's the rub. Which brings me back to my old hobby horse of keeping your independence till the day that you die.

'Don't worry Mom,' they say 'Of course we'll look after you!' And so I have no doubt they will, until it is a question of a child or wife of theirs needing something the same time as you do, and if the resources are not there for both there are no prizes for guessing who will come off second best always. And with us getting less and less attractive with old age, which seems to mean louder belches, noisier eating habits, involuntary sighs, radios or televisions on too loudly for everybody else in the house, forgetfulness leading to endless repetition... Good God, but I had better stop that list or I, too, will start to realise that with Eoin being another year older my turn is next.

Happy birthday Eoin and all our love!

Read Off the Altar (1994)

My son and daughter-in-law were read off the altar at Mass last Sunday — or so we told them when we got back to see could we take a rise out of them. But would you believe it? They both looked at us, blankly: they had never heard of the expression 'being read off the altar'. So then we had to explain how, long ago, if somebody had misbehaved themselves, like an un-married girl getting pregnant, the names were read off the altar as an object lesson to the rest of the congregation. Now, I per-sonally never saw this done, needless to mention, but such a thing was very strong in the folk memory and used as a dire warning to us growing up.

However, my young pair were read off the altar for another reason: they are having the Stations in a couple of weeks. Now

it did feel a bit odd to be sitting there and hear Eoin and Lisa
Kavanagh being read out for our Station area instead of Eoin
and Liz Kavanagh, similar as both sound. That really made us
feel the old pair. But then I sat back and relaxed because it
won't be me breaking my back cleaning up the place for the
next two weeks. Eoin and I will be involved all right. But we
won't be responsible, and that is a grand thought. Even grander
is the thought that I won't be responsible for the food either on
the day. I'll just be attending my Station Mass.

What a lot of Station Masses I have attended now since first I
came down here when my mother-in-law was still alive and I
took over from her. There was no question then of the woman's
name being read off the altar for the Stations. That only happened if she was a widow. And, as soon as her son grew up,
married or not, his name took over. It is still the same in farming
today. The only way a woman gets her name to the fore is when
she becomes a widow with young children. Always, even the
things that concern a woman as a joint operator of a farm, are
addressed to the man, be he husband or son. Did you ever see
things like notifications of meetings, come addressed to both
names. Is it any wonder then that so few women do go to farming
meetings when it is so obvious that they are not expected to
attend? Things are very slow to change.

It is only very recently that some of the clergy stopped being
gender blind and add in 'she' occasionally with the 'he'. I appreciate that. But it also gives the bright boys a chance to make
jokes. The other Sunday the Gospel was about the stoning of the
woman taken in adultery. And our good priest, being gender
conscious, in his sermon took it upon himself to re-phrase the
Gospel, reading it as: 'Let him, or her, who is without sin among
you cast the first stone.'

Outside in the chapel yard, after Mass, the ending of the lesson
was changed, however, by an inveterate teller of yarns, as he
retold the parable entirely, as follows:

'"Let him, or her, who is without sin cast the first stone,"
said Jesus, on his knees, his head bent. Then all at once this
great big rocker of a stone came whizzing through the air and
hit that poor woman, taken in adultery, slap bang in the middle
of her forehead. Jesus bent his head further to the ground, and

without turning around, said quite distinctly: "Oh Mother!"'

And, God forgive us, his listeners all laughed. The teller said it was the 'he or she' make him think of it. I suspect, however that probably it isn't even original, like his story of poor old St Joseph waking up after the marriage at Cana with the father and mother of a hangover. So he called on Mary to bring him up a jug of water: but then he quickly added, as the realisation struck him: 'But, what ever you do, don't leave the young fellow next, nigh, nor near it!', Joseph, of course, being in no humour for a hair of the dog that morning!

I know some people are shocked by any jokes about religion. I think, however, they are a very healthy sign. If a thing isn't worth joking about that means it has no significance in people's lives. Why else have we so many, many jokes, good, bad and indifferent, about sex? And I have no notion of telling you any of those, ever.

But I am telling my daughter-in-law not to be killing herself getting ready for the Stations. She was at my last one here before she ever got engaged to Eoin Óg, and at two or three others since she came here, so she knows the form. Actually, being a town girl, she things that the Stations are a marvellous idea: that is how she originally got to know all our immediate neighbours. She is also having a night station so that is also a help in the cleaning up. There will be no need to wash the gravel in front of the house as well as painting every window and door. They won't show in the dark.

In the times when Stations were more important than now there were people who cleaned the place to such an extent that the final thing was always to take up all the gravel in the front of the house, wash it in buckets of Lux liquid and then put it back again. I kid you not. And the smell of fresh paint would be overpowering. The men would always avoid leaning against the dresser less they get stuck to it. Thank God, as I said, that that is no longer my worry — unless some bright person thinks it a good idea for Mr and Mrs Eoin Kavanagh to have the Station in their own right and so put another six months onto the Stations round. Perish the thought.

Lisa and the Stations (1994)

Today we were bringing extra chairs into the hall in preparation for the Stations tomorrow night when suddenly Eoin said to Lisa, 'You have the beads ready for the giving out of the rosary here tomorrow night, I suppose?'

'The what?' the poor girl said in shock.

Hardly drawing a breath Eoin went on 'The mistress of the house always has to give out the rosary once three people have arrived, and keep it up, until the parish priest comes, and then she is the first into confession. 'Tis her place to do that. Well, you can't have the glory of being mistress of the house without some of the pain as well you know. This isn't a party, girl. This is religion. So it is the woman of the house's job to get the neighbours on the right track until the priest comes to take over.'

'You're joking,' said she, all unsure of herself, and she looked to me for confirmation. And I, with a totally straight face, enquired 'Is it the way you don't know the rosary, Lisa? I'll tell you what — Monday night, that's the Joyful Mysteries. I'll write them all out for you and you can keep the bit of paper in your hand and work off that — The Annunciation, The Visitation...' I stopped there lest I make a mistake myself...

'And, of course, you do know the start of the rosary? Don't you Lisa?'

She gave me a weak enough nod of the head. Eoin then asked her did she herself have a rosary beads? If not she could always borrow his, he said, or else, if the worst came to the worst, she could count on her fingers. She answered that there was a rosary beads around somewhere. I then compounded the story saying that giving out the rosary is always the job of the woman of the house, just as answering the Mass is the job of the man, until there is a son old enough to do this correctly.

'Do you mean Eoin Óg has to answer the Mass as well?' Lisa said, now in a right tizzy. 'God Almighty! All the time we wasted at that pre-marriage course — that's the sort of thing they should have been teaching us instead, especially us city girls getting married to farmers.'

Then, after a little reflection, she retorted with a return of her usual confidence, 'You are joking me aren't you — I know I never heard the rosary at the Stations last autumn...'

'But were you there before the priest?' interrupted Eoin, quick as a flash.

'No...,' she said, all doubtful once again. And then she was gone. We stayed with sorting out the furniture and, as we heard the back door slam, we knew she was gone to find her husband.

Sure enough, as he told us afterwards, she found him up in the calf shed and told him exactly what we were after telling her, word for word. Which of course made it dead easy for him. He simply agreed with every word we had said, adding that he was surprised she hadn't known that of course he would be serving the Mass. Who else did she think would do it?

Shortly afterwards she was on to her mother who said that she never heard of the giving out of the rosary before the Stations; that it was never done in her part of Galway. Lisa's father said he had never heard of it either, where he came from in West Cork, but added that customs varied a lot from place to place. He did also warn her, however, that we were probably winding her up and to take no notice. She, however, was taking a lot of notice. It is her first Station after all, so, of course she wants it to go right. And she is also having her family out to it and quite a few friends.

That is one thing the night Stations has done, made everything that much more social, more of a party in fact. It was quite a different thing in the past, with some of the past priests of this parish, I can tell you, who refused to have anything at all to do with night Stations. One particular man, long gone to his rest, thank God, always said half past eight Mass every morning in the parish church. So, he insisted that Station Masses all be at half past eight in the mornings as well. Lisa can't understand how we could possibly have managed that, having all the cows milked, calves attended to, fires lit, and all the rest of it done. Well we managed it all right, by being up at four o'clock in the morning. It was as simple as that. Also, only one representative from each house then came, not both husband and wife which is the way quite regularly now. And it was nothing fancier than two boiled eggs for everyone, just so long as the hens were still laying. If not, only some got the second egg and us children got just the top off the egg and were grateful. The big job was not to have the eggs runny or like bullets. With a lot of women helpers in the kitchen that wasn't always as easy as it seemed.

Lisa's friends are all making cakes and stuff for her so I think that we are in for a good feed: usually there are a lot of leftovers after the Stations. Eoin Óg did break the truth to Lisa when he came in and found her hammering away at a slab of pastry, all put out about giving out the rosary, and not at all upset about cooking food for anything up to forty people. Well, he said, he had to live with her, when we were at him later as to why didn't he wait to see if Lisa really would lead the neighbours in the rosary on the night. Everybody might be convinced all right that we had a resident saint on our hands. But Lisa threatened her husband that if she found it was all a joke she would be gone, on the spot, and we could have our Stations all by ourselves!

When she found out the truth, however, from Eoin Óg, she came back in to her father-in-law, all smiles, as he rested awhile. She, however, now had a reel of Sellotape behind her back. And, coming at Eoin from behind, Lisa taped over Eoin's mouth, fast, with two or three bits of Sellotape and told him, if he knew what was good for him, he'd keep that on until the Stations were well and truly over.

But I have my doubts if he'll get off as easy as all that, with April the first only five weeks away. If I know Lisa she is already plotting her revenge. And I had better mind my own back as well because she says that I could at least have warned her.... But I do so enjoy a bit of life around the house once more — and the keeping up of all the old customs.

February Fill-Dyke (1995)

February fill-dyke this month was called when I was young and how true it is again this year. We will be all glad to see the back of it and that's for sure. We live half way up a hill, so at least the water rushes past us on its way down to the valley and then out to sea. But I don't know how often I have looked out my bedroom window in the mornings and seen swans swimming on what should be fields in the valley below. I have been strongly tempted to shut the curtains again and go back into bed and pull the covers over my head. But the habits of a lifetime are hard to break and I always get up when I wake up, even though it is others who now have to milk the cows and feed the calves.

They are the ones who are suffering most and I often see them coming in like drowned rats and frozen with the cold. Luckily enough we still have plenty of silage and straw left, unless this rain never stops, so there isn't that worry on top of everything else. We haven't had the cows out to grass yet, and no immediate hope of that either with the condition the land is in. But with silage enough in the pits, and straw enough for the straw chopper to bed the cubicles twice weekly, that means we can sleep at night.

I heard a lovely one on the radio coming home from college the other night when I was fiddling with the radio knobs and tuned into a farming programme by accident on one of the local stations. This man said that the day you finish up with no silage in your yards, that is the day you have lost control of your grassland management. The point he was making was that you must always have something in your yards for the unexpected bad weather, whatever month of the year it is, when cows are better off in than out ploughing up the fields. Silage in the pits is better than money in the bank, he said. I saved up that one about the day you have no silage in your pits is the day you have lost control of your grassland management to tell them when I got home. And, as the rain still came pelting down next day, I heard Eoin Óg on the phone booking the silage contractor for this year's cut, for at least the same number of acres as last year and hopefully a few more he said.

It is hard to imagine cutting silage again though, with conditions the way they are at the moment. It is at least two weeks now since, at the instigation of our parish priest, we all said three Hail Mary's at the end of Mass for a change in the weather. On the way out, however, one old man remarked that we may as well be idle until the new moon in March. He wasn't having any of this blind faith business. He was relying on a lifetime's observation of the weather instead. And, true enough, I do remember it always being said that changes only came with the new moon. I don't know if there is any scientific basis or not for that belief. But I, for one, am looking forward to the new moon.

There has to be a change then surely, if we are not to sink into the sea altogether. Wasn't there another old yarn about Ireland not being consumed by fires at the end of the world, like every place else, because it would have sunk into the sea by then? And didn't St Malachy prophesy that the end of the world would be nigh when we couldn't distinguish the seasons, winter from summer, except by the leaves on the trees? Eoin says it is raining virtually non stop since last Summer, so I don't know.

Anyway I said the three Hail Mary's with the best of them at Mass, but, ever before my old neighbour put in his tuppence worth, the devil tempted me with the memory of the last time I heard prayers for fine weather. Now that bishop, not of this diocese I hasten to add, ordered prayers for fine weather to be said at every Mass one Sunday early last April. We happened to be at Mass in that diocese on our way somewhere else. Coming out, in the queue at the doorway, I happened to remark to a total stranger what a lovely thing it was, a bishop caring for the farmers, and the weather we'd all been having lately. I then added that we had had nothing like that from our man.

'Maybe that's true enough' said he, 'But I think our cute bucko must have had a quick squint at the weather forecast last night, because I hear they gave a great story altogether for the coming week...'

And, sure enough, even though it was still raining away as we left the church it soon turned into a lovely day and the weather did improve dramatically from that Sunday on, what-ever the real reason was for that.

To get back to February fill-dyke, however, the roads around here are in a shocking state altogether after the weather. Some of them are like driving up a river bed. Now ours isn't bad at all for the very simple reason that we, and a neighbour on the other side, clear our own dykes regularly between us and the main road, just to keep the floods off the road itself. God be with the days when there were roadmen employed to do nothing but that. They may not have been overworked with their shovels all winter on their constant round of dyke cleaning — one of my sons used to constantly remark on them breast feeding their shovels at regular intervals. The roads, however, were in a much better state as a result of even their minimal care. Sure it only stands to reason that floods of water will literally tear chunks and lumps out of the road surface if they are allowed to run over it unchecked. And all it takes is a few minutes, even with the heel of your boot, to free the obstruction in a dyke that is forcing the flood water onto the road.

We, as a nation, are not the best when it comes to self-help I fear, always saying that that is the County Council's job, looking after the roads around us. And you would want to be careful, it appears, before you take on the job of fixing any major potholes. In desperation, with the worst potholes outside our place, we resorted to concrete. But we were quickly made aware that if any accident happened there it is we who could be sued and not the County Council. And removing the concrete again would not absolve, since it could be argued that it was us, or our agents, who had made the pothole in our attempts to remove all the concrete. Talk about being between a rock and a hard place.

So now I'm in half a mind about asking one of the sons to do his usual cute trick of driving up and down our hill with one set of the tractor wheels in the dyke, to give a grand clear run to the rainwater. The next person to dyke themselves on our narrow road, which happens on regular occasions, if they knew that, might then decide to sue on the flimsy grounds that we had deepened the dyke. And, with the general carry on in our law courts at the moment, they'll probably get away with it too.

MARCH

Echoes from the Past (1978)

How times change! Lady's Day is almost upon us and it may as well be nothing. Only the older ones among us will have even the vaguest of folk memories of the hiring of labour on Lady's Day, 25 March. This used to be the day around here when the bargains for the year were made. My sons, however, showed scant interest when, to fill a really wet and cold afternoon, I showed them some of their great-grandmother's contracts with her farm workers — and I also tried to tell them what a great woman she was for her times.

She was a second wife whose husband then upped and died on her when she had produced three sons and one daughter in quick succession and was pregnant as well with Eoin's father. Her husband got pneumonia, and, as was so often the case in those days, he did not survive the crisis. I got my sons' attention all right when I next told them that my grandfather was the one who was asked to shave their Dad's grandfather, in preparation for the wake in the house. That was supposed to be the greatest mark of honour and respect. Others, who considered themselves closer, took umbrage at the new widow woman's choice to perform this last task. In one particular case a family feud went on for years as a result.

The seeds of another family feud also began with that ceremonial shave, however, one that was to affect Eoin and myself years later. In the course of time, my grandmother began to get very resentful of the attention and help her husband still continued to give the widow bringing up her young family on her own. Angry words were exchanged and the bitterness extended onto some of the next generation. My godmother, my father's sister, disowned me on the spot when I decided to marry Eoin, never really speaking to me again in all the years since. I doubt if she will remember me in her will either, even though she has neither chick nor child, nor, indeed, any other godchild, to her name.

This sort of detail was what the boys wanted to hear even though I then drew them back to the topic in hand by asking them what the date, the twenty fifth of March, meant to them. My eldest, quickly enough said that it was the day of the Annunciation, when the angel told Mary she was going to have a baby — he is at least learning some religion at his boarding school even though, this week, we had some difficulty in getting him to go to confession with the rest of us, to make his Easter duty.

Seamus, however, abruptly interrupted that explanation. 'The twenty fifth of March — of course that's the date we always let the bulls off to the cows, Mom — if we did it any earlier, sure we'd have them calving down at Christmastime and that's better kept free since there's only Dad and myself here those days...and we can't do everything between us! And we must make the most of the January and February bonus — sure there's nothing at all extra for milk delivered in December....'

He's our farmer son all right, the practical one, and the making of a fine male chauvinist as well, if I don't watch out. Who does he think looks after the calves, and often the cows as well, even when the workmen are back from their Christmas break and he's gone back to school? But, before I got into that, his casual juxtaposition of the Annunciation, and the bulls being left off out to the cows, did strike me as very funny, even if faintly blasphemous. He is quite right however. The gestation period is the same for cows as it is for humans, nine months and ten days. So, 25 March does bring us bang on to 1 January and not Christmas day. I wonder was it Mary, or the Angel Gabriel, who got their dates slightly wrong?

Eoin's grandmother had no such difficulty in getting help during the Christmas holiday period. The contracts she made with her workers are kept in her account book, which I cherish, and which she called her 'Labour Account Book'. In it she kept track of all the money forwarded to the men and women in her employment. The men were paid on a weekly basis but the women only quarterly. It makes fascinating reading now. Some took their full money every week. Some thrifty souls merited the entry 'left down five days 5s 0d — two days 2s 0d', and so on. Other poor souls were always in debt by the end of the quarter when it appears there was always a grand totalling of the columns. This fact is not surprising really because, in 1891, a pair of boots cost them seven shillings. So a man had to work a seven-day week to buy himself a pair of boots for his feet. That grandmother obviously did the buying for them and then stopped it out of their money. For the maid 'stuff for aprons' came to 3s 5d and a corset was 2s 0d.

These girls had contracted for six pounds for the full year in question, 25 March 1891 to 25 March 1892. So, when they had to pay for even their own aprons, how could there be much left for them at the end of each quarter. Each item purchased was carefully noted in the account book, as were the fines for any item broken. A chamber pot was debited at 2s 0d, the same as a corset, and I would love to know just how that chamber pot got broken in the emptying of same, probably on the dung heap in the yard, the usual spot in my earliest memories.

Even the shilling advance for the Station dues the morning of the Stations here in the house, was duly noted. Another entry read 'to attend his grandfather's funeral, 5s 0d — one day out of his time 1s 0d.' Eoin's grandmother was a hard-headed business woman in the running of her farm, it seems. There was no such thing as a day off work to go to a family funeral in those days.

The employees' families often called on her for their share of their son's or daughter's pay as well Quite often the entries read — 'to mother 5s 0d', or 'to father '2s 0d'. The mothers calling always seemed to get more than the fathers. I wouldn't say that this grandmother had much time for feckless men. Unfortunately there isn't even a hint as to whether they got as much as they asked for, or did the grandmother decide what was right. Some of the entries do have more detail though. One, on 11 October 1902, reads:

'Nora Daly sailed to America this morning. Owing to me 2s 9d and she did no work for me yesterday.'

Those must have been hard times. So much can be read between the lines. I do wonder what became of this Nora Daly in
America because she, in all the account book, is the only person
who seems to have got the better of Eoin's grandmother. Her
children, or indeed great-grandchildren, may indeed have done
very well for themselves in America. I would dearly love to
know and only hope that some day her descendants come
around looking for their roots.

I have spent many hours poring over the entries in this book.
The most fascinating bits, however, are the Lady Day agreements tucked here and there among the pages. They seem so
very far away from the present day labour situation. Everything, then, was really spelt out for both sides. I am amused to
note that Margaret Kavanagh was just as reluctant in her day to
feed all and sundry as I am today. In most of the agreements she
firmly stipulated 'and without diet'. One such typical agreement, including those words, reads as follows:

Memorandum of agreement between Mgt J. Kavanagh
and John Linehan.

He is to work for me, as farm labourer, from March 25,
1901 to March 25, 1902, at the rate of seven shillings per
week, without diet. He is to do this work cheerfully and
willingly. He is to attend on Sundays and all Holy days to
the feeding of cattle and horses.

His wife is to work when required, on the farm or otherwise, binding and about turnips and mangolds, and for
milking the cows when required, or assistance in the house,
at the rate of eight pence a day.

He will get as reward for faithful service, five drills of
potatoes planted and tilled in the long field and a half ton of
coal at Christmas.

His sister, Annie, is to bind during the harvest, at one
shilling a day.

His daughter, Ellie, is to work as domestic servant in the
house at six pounds a year.

Signed by Margaret J. Kavanagh
+ John Linehan, his mark

All this was duly legally witnessed, and a sixpenny stamp affixed, which seems extraordinarily high when poor old Mrs Linehan was only getting eight pence for a full day's work. The legal boys and the government got the fat and the lean of it in those days too.

Women certainly did not account for much those days. All of John Linehan's womenfolk were lumped in with him in his agreement, with none of them seemingly able to read or write. And they did not even get the chance to put their marks with his. Poor Mrs Linehan was given neither the courtesy of that title nor her Christian name. And I do wonder why she was considered to be worth so much less that her sister-in-law? Too much worn out with child birth, no doubt, to be of much use in either field or house and Eoin's grandmother made sure of her side of the bargain. She was some operator. She was also a fine figure of a woman, it seems. No wonder my grandmother got jealous of all the assistance being rendered to her by my grandfather.

Not that Eoin's grandmother needed that much assistance, I believe, because soon her stepson, the only child of the first marriage, was gone, apprenticed to a business in the city at barely fourteen years of age. Her own eldest son was then semi-fostered by childless relatives, rarely returned home, and she got on with the business of running the farm, getting another farm of land to rent from the landlord, and soon extended her entrepreneurial skills to taking out contracts for road making and providing a charabanc service joining up this area to the nearest railway station. But then she was a young widow. And the only women to wrest power in the Ireland of those days were widows with only young children, or reverend mothers. And I'd better watch my sons because I can see that inherited tendency to grab control coming out very much now that they are in their teens.

No Longer an Easy Mark (1985)

Do you know that something struck me the other day and that is that we no longer have hordes of ticket sellers coming to our door. So the word really must be out, the mark on the avenue piers, or something. The tinkers were supposed to do that, weren't they, leave a mark for the next lot, to distinguish the houses that it was not worth while even trying? If there really is such a mark on our place, and I could only discover it, then I'd patent it and make good money selling it to everybody else.

For years I found it well nigh impossible to turn anyone away empty-handed at my door especially when they were all for good causes. I used to persuade myself that we'd never miss the pound note, my usual donation, and we might even win something. We never won a single thing, however, and the pound note was eyed disdainfully by my callers long before the pound notes themselves disappeared. It soon became a pound a line and, not only that, but I would always be casually shown a card with all my neighbours having bought a lot more lines than just the one I proposed to purchase.

All ticket sellers must be first sent on sales courses on how to manipulate people I have decided. Not alone are you put on guilt trips by disabled people collecting for the disabled but they also play on our desire not to appear to be mean. Even the beggars on the street do that by salting their collection cap with a pound or too. How then can you throw a copper on something that only contains silver? And wasn't there the story going the rounds how Ian Paisley only wants a silent collection and sends around big tin buckets to ensure this?

And what about the GAA clubs, parish building funds, and the like, who were running that spate of demands, for hundred pound tickets no less, for the prize of a fancy car. Then the men appearing at our door were people we knew and so we were rightly expected to find it hard to say no. Whatever about supporting your own parish, however, it becomes a bit much of a thing when you are expected to help build churches and GAA halls elsewhere as well. Needless to mention we never won a car or anything remotely like it.

The whole thing was more than getting us down with not a week going by without someone or other at our door for one cause or another. Then the final crunch came late one dark winters night. We were in bed, with all the lights out, when a strange car drove up the front and stopped. We heard the ca doors slam and two sets of footsteps coming to the front door. We sat up in panic as somebody coming to your door after eleven at night can only mean trouble. Eoin grabbed his trousers, and the shotgun, which lives behind our bedroom door. The doorbell rang but Eoin stuck his head and the now loaded gun out the window instead and shouted out, 'Who's there?' He had spotted that it wasn't a Garda car, which is every parent's midnight fear.

A man's voice replied that they were only so-and-so and so-and-so and that they were selling tickets for this great draw and were so sorry for disturbing us but the closing date was —. They got no further, needless to say, as they were told in quite forceful language what they could do with themselves and their tickets and what would happen to them if they did not get themselves off our property quickly. Eoin was fit to be tied and it was hard to blame him for that. Getting back to sleep was well nigh impossible too, at least until the sons were in. There and then we determined that never again would we give any-thing to anybody calling at the house.

It would have to be a blanket refusal if this was to work. So I was told that there were to be no exceptions at all, not even when I tentatively mentioned the two groups of nuns and the priests I inherited from his aunt Mary when I came to this place. They have been getting donations here, for over half a century at least, so what was I to do about them? I could see myself telling all the newer ones all right that we never gave anything to anybody at the door, but no way could I see myself doing that to others, especially that old, old brother who always gave us the medals of St Benedict to put up in the cow byre. God love him in his bare sandalled feet. He never moved with the times and the parlour to him was where I gave him a cup of tea and not where our cows are milked. He, or his look alike, was the very one who used to try to put his skull cap on the heads of my sons so as to ensure they got a vocation. That never worked, whatever about the medals of St Benedict doing any good for the cows!

He, or his look alike, was the very one who used to try to put his skull cap on the heads of my sons so as to ensure they got a vocation. That never worked, whatever about the medals of St Benedict!

But saying no to everybody else did work. Mind you it was not easy. I had to say no to all those I had encouraged over the years. You know how it is, give something one year and they are back again the next when you have to give again and so it goes on. But it also worked in reverse. By saying no just that one year they stopped coming back. Not one returned to try if my resolve had weakened. And, what is more important, no new collectors appeared ever since. Which makes me strongly suspect some sort of list being in existence somewhere, of easy marks, which is circulated somehow among charity collectors. Well, that notion, be it right or wrong, is a lot more feasible these days than marks on entrances, now isn't it?

Getting a really cross dog may also be far more feasible than trusting to one's ability to give a blanket no at the door. I retained more of my retinue of collectors at my front door than I really want. But, with a really cross dog on the loose, maybe they'd be deterred from ringing my bell.

Don't Just Get Mad — Get Even (1992)

'You don't know you are living,' said Eoin to Pádraig when they came with the news, and the request for baby minding. 'In my day it was hard enough even to get the few days off for the Spring Show, and here you are...' He tapered off lest he say too much. You see Pádraig and Sara had been at some charity table quiz the night before and Pádraig had won them a week for two in Tenerife, to be taken before the end of the month. And of course it is only a few weeks since they were last off on holidays, and again we had the children. So I suppose Eoin rightly felt it was fine for them to be able to just pack up like that and the farm and everything else would just go on.

Me, I was so delighted that this son of mine, who never shone at school, was able to take the top prize like that. Modestly enough he said that the questions just fell his way. But I was proud out of him, as indeed was his wife. So why did it all warrant that 'they don't know they are living' feeling, that Eoin and I so often get about our family, despite ourselves. Pure jealousy I dare say is what is wrong with us. Our living was often so hard and tough that it kills us to see them having it so easy. Whenever we see them, as we would call it, 'throwing money away', it bothers us at some extraordinarily deep level. OK, they won this holiday, but the week will cost them plenty for all that. But, as it isn't out of our pocket the money is coming, why are we worrying?

I am beginning to wonder is our particular form of begrudgery because we are farming parents? Farmers who hand over their means of livelihood to their children never seem to totally let go, to really call it a day. They feel, somehow way down in their subconscious, that their children owe them a debt that can never be paid off, and that's why they don't have to fully let go. The young people, after all, only have what they have because of the hard work, and the doing without, of those who went before them. And, at times, that generation wonder if they weren't all kinds of fools to have been always planning for the future of the family and not living in the present as others seemed to do, and be none the worse for it either. That's where the jealousy and the begrudgery comes in. And the women feel it far worse than the men. The land, the sheds, and even the cows are a visible reminder to the men, after they hand over, that their work wasn't all in vain. But all the women I know, who handed over their houses, found that the first thing the new woman did was to put her own stamp on the place by changing everything about. And that hurts.

I know, because during the week we met up with some old friends of ours and the conversation, naturally enough, turned to our respective families. They, like us, are counting grandchildren and they, although about ten years ahead of us, are still negotiating relationships with in-laws. I was somewhat wryly amused to hear my friend Mary complain that her daughter-in-law was a great girl and all that, but not alone had she thrown out the perfectly good curtains Mary had left after her when she and Tom had moved out to their bungalow, but their replacements had just been dumped as well.

'I saw them with my own eyes out with the rubbish. And I wouldn't mind so much,' said Mary, 'but I had to make do for many's the long year with the curtains that were in the place when I came there.'

Not surprisingly Mary and I had a great time deciding what was wrong with the next generation. The present generation have no idea of the times when farmers had nothing and were nobody. Therein lies the nub of the matter. No matter how hard the next generation think they have things now they are all vastly better off than we were at their stage of life. They can afford things we only dreamed of possessing, like fully fitted kitchens and carpets wall to wall.

And they consider everything to have a 'best before date', after which practically anything can be happily dumped. There is no longer the wearing out even of clothes, first for Mass and best wear, then second best wear, and finally about the yard when the zips had just about given up in the skirts but the cross-over apron covered a multitude. Even our curtains, as Mary reminded me, went from the parlour to the bedrooms before they hit the rag bag, or served as clothes for the floor or the sink. 'My lassie buys J-Cloths for that, and special yellow dusters,' added Mary.

There is no doubt but this new generation is the disposable generation. Still what difference does that make really just so long as they do not apply that philosophy to their marriage partners?

But you know something that generation may have to complain about, and that is that the likes of Mary and myself are living far too long. Both Mary and I had our mothers-in-law to deal with for a very short period of years before they died and neither of us had a father-in-law. So what we did with the family curtains after that affected nobody really. But Mary's daughter-in-law, and possibly mine too, could well be mothers-in-law themselves before they see the last of us, and get rid of the feel of us perpetually looking over their shoulders.

If I was to be really cynical I could say that the car sticker I once saw could well be modified for the likes of Mary and others:

DON'T JUST GET MAD: GET EVEN.
LIVE LONG ENOUGH TO BE A BURDEN ON YOUR
CHILDREN ... *AND YOUR DAUGHTERS-IN-LAW.*

Let Ye Have At It So (March 93)

'Let ye have at it so!' Didn't I myself say that to my sons during the week when we disagreed over putting the calves out to grass, and, once the words were out of my mouth, all sorts of memories came flooding back to me of another time and another age.

It is years and years since I first heard that expression. I was barely into my teens when my father died, leaving my mother to cope with all of us, and run a farm as well. Of course, I was much too young to realise the enormity of that fact, being too devastated by my own loss, as well as having no idea of what it was like for a woman, never used to it, being suddenly cata-pulted into decision making of all sorts. That was before the days of farm advisers, farm contractors, farm publications and all the other sources of farming advice today. Experience then was the only guideline on everything. Sons learned from their fathers and anybody coming to farming, as a few did, with 'book-learning', were mocked for their strange activities when farmers gathered to talk.

Tractors were a rare enough commodity too. My father, however, was always mad on machinery, so we had two trac-tors no less, a Massey Ferguson and one that ran on cleat-tracks, like a tank. He also had the first combine harvester, ever, to come into this area. I well remember the masses of men crossing the fields, every fine day, coming to see this wonder at work. My elder brother and I were usually on the platform looking after the bags, packing in the grain by catching up the bags and shaking them as they filled. Then, with a pull of a lever, the grain was directed down a new chute while we tightly tied the mouth of the full sack and child-handled it out onto the sack-chute.

It was quite hard work while the combine went, and very boring during the constant repairs. So we made up this song which we sang, loudly, once we were sure Dadda was safely out of earshot:

There was a farmer had a combine, ee-i ee-i o,
With a break break here, and a break break there,
Here a break, there a break, everywhere a break break…

And so we went on, verse after verse after verse. How cross the poor man used to get if anybody came to see his new acquisition, just when something had gone wrong, as it frequently did. But he always managed to greet them with a welcoming smile as if everything was fine. All that we incorporated into our song.

Then, early the following January, Dadda died suddenly. The tractors were sold, as were the combine and the rest of the machinery too because of nobody there to manage it. It was back to horse power for everything, plus of course woman and child power. My uncle, her brother, was my mother's only support really, but he lived quite far away. The workman, no matter what she asked him, always had the one stock answer, 'I'll lave it to yourself Ma'am,' — which wasn't a great deal of good to her.

The neighbours were great though, at the beginning, with advice which was very necessary. But once my mother found her feet, and her capability, she had considerable difficulty in having her word final. Those neighbouring men always had some reason as to why her decisions were invariably all wrong. Finally, she used to insist on doing things her way. Then, there was one particular man, when things first came to an impasse with him over whether or not a field of hay was fit to cock, who said to her 'let ye have at it so!' as he walked out of the field in a blazing temper. Now, with hindsight, that may seem to be a thing of nothing. But picture a woman never in all her life having to make farming decisions of any sort suddenly having to decide whether or not grass was dry enough to put up into cocks and the whole winter feed for the cows depending on this crop of hay. And then the male neighbour who had been a tower of strength, as well as a source of very necessary manpower, stalking off because she questioned his judgement about the fitness of a crop. We were all there, with our pikes, making those cocks well into the night even though the neighbour had said that we would have to shake it all out again if the stuff heated, and once was bad enough to be doing it. Anyway the day stayed fine, the rain only coming in over the hill as we finished. We developed blisters on our hands. But the field was cocked. And it was perfect hay.

Months later when it was being fed to the cows that neighbour took a fist of it, looked at it, felt it, smelt it, and said, grudgingly,

'Ignorance is a great thing after all. Only somebody really ignorant would have cocked that hay on that day, and look at it now, the finest hay I ever did see in my life.'

Now you have no idea of what a big 'spake' that was. Here was a man, who, by definition, had to know everything, admitting in a sideways fashion that the poor widow woman had actually been right. And ever after, until there was no further need for his watchful eye on our farm, whenever anything arose and my mother had an opinion of her own he used to just cast his eyes up to heaven and say to her 'Let ye have at it so!' And so she did, with considerable success. But there was a certain wisdom in that man's acceptance of her hard won independence of thought. He had done his best and knew when he was defeated. He never stalked out of a field again on her. But that saying of his was a constant oblique expression of his disapproval.

Now I too need to save face with my sons when I know I'm beaten, though I still feel I know best. 'Let ye have at it so.' I said about putting the calves out to grass so early in the year and with heavy rain forecast. Doubtless I will say that again and again about lots of things even if not using those exact same words. I wonder, however, if I will ever become sufficiently detached to opt out, like that workman of my mother's half a century ago, and invariably say, 'I'll leave it to yourself, son', when any farming decision needs to be made.

Any Day at All! (1997)

Earlier this week I got an urgent phone call from Sara to know would I collect Nicole from playschool and to please keep her until three o'clock when Michaella was collected from her school, the reason being that she and Pádraig were badly delayed in town. I like to get calls like that because it is good to be needed occasionally by the self-sufficient generation of today. So, I said that of course I'd collect Michaella as well at three, if that was any help, and I'd feed them and do

Michaella's lessons with her as well. I know I was quite busy myself when the call came, but it wasn't with anything that couldn't wait for another day. My granddaughters' childhood is slipping by all too quickly on me as it is.

Nicole has just started going to playschool for two days a week. I was interested to see how this child would react when I went to pick her up for the first time. I still treasure the way Michaella's face would always light up with sheer and absolute delight on seeing me come unexpectedly for her at playschool. But, as I keep on saying, Nicole is a very different kettle of fish.

She is two and three-quarters, but way more advanced than her big sister was at the same age. Of course that comes with having an older sister to play with. I am fascinated by the different characteristics already so evident in my two grand-daughters. Nicole is one determined young woman. She stands four square, looks one in the eye and says exactly what she thinks and wants. She gives no quarter that lady. And we have no doubt precisely which member of the family she takes after!

When Sara phoned, and I was really busy, Eoin still said that I had better go for Nicole myself, even though he was only sitting there reading the paper at the time. This was quite unlike Eoin, for I may as well tell you that Nicole is his special pet. He knocks great amusement out of her independent ways and sayings. But, times being what they are, Eoin said that he would feel very uncomfortable if Nicole should suddenly decide that she did not want to go with her grandfather after all. At that age one can never be sure how a child will react when con-fronted with the unexpected and nobody but her mother has picked her up so far from playschool.

Never do I remember such a reaction from Eoin before, so I told him that he is watching far too many television pro-grammes and reading too much in the papers about the awful things that happen. He retorted that the nursery school teacher might not remember him since he had so rarely collected Michaella anyway, so she would be perfectly right not to let a small girl go off with a strange man, especially if that small girl created a fuss. We both knew, only too well, that Nicole is quite capable of doing just that if the notion takes her. There is no doubt that life must have become horribly complicated for many men if such a thought crosses the mind of a grandfather like Eoin living in rural Ireland.

In fact, when I arrived, Nicole, while she did deign to recognise me, was determined not to come with me until she had fully finished her puzzle. Indeed, she did not seem all that enamoured at all to see me, so concentrated was she on the task in hand. This was in very sharp contrast to how Michaella behaved when I'd pick her up there. Her little face used to just light up at the sight of me and she'd leave anything and everybody to run into my waiting arms.

But the magic word 'shop' whispered in Nicole's ear, soon changed her tune and made her accept the correct puzzle pieces — she had already pushed away my hand forcibly when I tried to speed up its completion. Then she took my hand all right and refused to stop even to put on her coat on our way out. She was all chat to me in the car, about her morning, and home, even to the extent of giving me one of the drawings she had made for her mother. She told me that was to go on the wall in my house, 'with Ka's'. I keep a permanent art gallery of Michaella's drawings in the kitchen.

Michaella's name has been shortened by her sister to Ka, which well may stick as a pet name, since I have heard both parents use it when talking to Nicole of her big sister. A son of mine, who had best be nameless for the sake of peace in this house, went through all his national school days with the name of Boo-Boo. An older brother called him that at home, his approximation of baby. And my name of Diyee has stuck very firmly to me since Michaella first insisted that that was my name, she was having none of the usual names for grandmother. It was years before we discovered this was her version of darling. To the rest of my grandchildren I am Grandma, Granny and Gran, which were obviously their parents' choice since unfortunately they are all far away to even know me properly, or I them. But I have a special weakness for the title Diyee.

Nicole duly made her visit to the shop, ate all I bought her, and a fine lunch as well. She then demanded the Bambi video to be put on. This suited me to perfection since she was asleep on the couch in five minutes flat. So I was free for my own affairs until I collected Michaella and made yet another trip to the shop. Then we all ate another dinner as well, with the mashed potatoes made into castles, and, since it was raining, put on another video which we all watched together, Nicole taking over my lap.

Nicole was never one for the hugs and kisses that Michaella thrived on. However, that evening, while sitting on my lap, she unexpectedly put her two hands on my face, one on each side, and gently felt up and down the contours, exactly as I remember Michaella doing to me one morning, after she had got into our bed at some ungodly hour in the dark. It was as though at the time each of them was imprinting my features on their memories, with incredibly soft and gentle touches, totally unsolicited caresses.

And I felt a renewed surge of love for my girls, my granddaughters, my flesh and blood. That is one thing about the grandchildren one sees regularly: they keep on adding deposits of love to their accounts in your heart, even if they are inclined to take over your life utterly and completely when they are visiting.

When, very much later, Sara left with my two little pets, who really did not want to go at all and only consented to stir when I carried Nicole out to the car while holding Missy's hand, and I personally tied on both safety belts. I told Sara that I had had a truly great day with them, and any time at all she wanted her girls picked up, to just say the word, and I'd be there. But she, while thanking me, replied by saying that any day at all that I wanted them, for me to just say the word!

So, do you think that we are a typical modern mother and daughter-in-law caught in a stalemate situation of being careful of never treading on each other toes that neither us fully satisfied as a consequence?

APRIL

How Will J. R. Do? (1981)

A long-ago neighbour of ours, when something tickled her
fancy, always said that a good laugh was every bit as good for a
person as a dose of salts. Yet, she left nothing to chance and still
went for the ceremonial dosing of her children with Syrup of
Figs, or an infusion of senna pods, on a weekly basis. Eoin, too,
also had to take his weekly spoonful of Syrup of Figs during his
childhood, and to this day hates the very thought of figs in any
form. I was reminded of all that, last night, by a very odd association of thoughts, of bulls and figs, just before I went to sleep.
So I idly traced back my sequence of thoughts, something that
often amuses me in quiet moments. Then it was all clear because
we had left two bulls out to the cows yesterday morning, and I
also checked later on in the day to see if any figs had survived
the winter on my Brown Turkey fig, a new acquisition planted
last year against the warmest wall I could manage. None had.
But then I started thinking of how Eoin and I laughed last
evening when I just had to call him out from the milking parlour.
Thus I finished up with old Annie and her weekly dosing of
Syrup of Figs.

You see, being breeding season again, the bulls are running
with the cows once more in turn. Having a fair few cows, and
increasing the numbers every year, we have several bulls who
get their days on and days off-duty. We never have any trouble
with them, running together in pairs as they do, because, after
their first posturing, they are then distracted by all the cows
urgently needing their services. You'd laugh to see them, when

freshly left off in the mornings, serving one cow, with a weather eye open for all other cows in heat heading off out to grass. And, when the bulls do reach the field, sometimes also doing the job on the way, they then seem to take up different territories, too busy about their business to take much notice of each other, or us either.

We are constantly wary of bulls, however, no matter when, where or even how quiet they have been in the past. They are not to trusted no matter how gentle they seem. In the pre-breeding season, when kept away from all female company, they get very restive indeed while waiting for the green light to get at their harem, who, no doubt, scent the very air with their desire and their lesbian tendencies, in want of the real thing. You wouldn't want to go next nor near the bulls' yards during this period. We feed them only over their confining walls.

The oldest bull of them all, 007, freeze-branded as such at the insistence of the lads, when the cows were first being branded two years ago, is by far the most vocal, and dangerous. He, like James Bond, has well lived up to his name, being active in every way. The roars of him, these past weeks, at any signs of human activity, have really been something. There is no way anybody in their right mind would go near him, except, per-haps, to watch in amusement as his frustration leads him to attack the very walls of his enclosure after much pawing the ground and tossing of his bedding up in the air with his horns.

The new, young, and as yet untried bull with him these past weeks, for company, used to look in amazement at him, perhaps wondering if 007 knew something he didn't. That is one of the many lessons Eoin brought back with him from his trip to New Zealand, firstly, that it is possible to run several bulls together with the cows and that they don't half kill each other, and secondly, that bulls are much safer during their period of deprivation, if they have company. A lot of homosexual activity goes on all right. But then, doesn't it always, even with a field of bullocks? The pecking order was established very fast with these bulls locked up together. 007 is the top bull, in every sense of the word.

Eoin has been talking very seriously of getting rid of old 007 altogether, as he was making such a nuisance of himself. Yet, because he has 'thrown' such great calves, of both sexes, he was given a temporary reprieve until we have another crop of replacement heifers from him. However, on the day he was put to this work, we took the precaution of letting the whole herd down, to mill around his yard, before opening his gate to let him off. Then he was out with a great bound, as Eoin scuttled away, keeping several cows between them until he, Eoin, was over another gate and safe. Not that 007 took the slightest notice really as he took off in bucks, leaps and 'fouches'. In his sexual excitement he scattered even the willing cows. He went off, no bother, out to grass with all his lady friends, the young bull somewhat sheepishly bringing up the rear. Eoin was very worried, however, about how we were to make the change-over the following morning milking. John-Boy was then to have his turn again, with his apprentice in tow. All day long Eoin was crossing his bridges before he ever met them, planning his strategies if 007 came into the parlour with the cows, or if he stayed in the collecting yard to the very end.

Still I was the one who went for the cows last evening, with Eoin's dire warnings ringing in my ears. I was quite confident, however, since I always stay within easy reach of an electric fence if ever all the cows do not come out of the field by themselves and I have to go in after them. Usually though, the cows know milking time even better than ourselves. The boss cows always gather at the gap ahead of time so that they can keep their dominant position, being first into the milking parlour and so out first as well, to fresh grass after milking. Actually, it was the electric fence wire that saved me the one and only time I was ever chased by a bull.

That same day I had been in town, shopping, and as usual, got somewhat delayed. So, to speed things up, knowing I was on cow duty that afternoon, on my way home I drove straight to the field to bring in the cows. All went fine, as usual, until suddenly, for no reason at all, the bull suddenly took after me. Fortunately, I was right near the side fence wire, so I hopped over it, mighty fast, high heels, summer dress, and all. I then found the breath to roar at the still charging bull. Immediately he heard my voice giving out to him, he skidded to a halt, with a ridiculously surprised expression on his face. The poor devil had never recognised me in my city get-up. He had never seen me in a frock before, after all, only in pants. He obviously thought that he was chasing off some alien creature, never having seen a frock in his life. You never saw anything like the ashamed way he turned on his heels and left me, to meekly follow the cows. I had to smile to myself, while vowing never again to be so stupid. It just went to show, anyway, that it really does pay to 'talk to the animals', which I do, constantly.

But, to get back to 007, yesterday afternoon I never even noticed him passing me by in the middle of the cows. He came into the parlour all right while we were milking but caused no trouble at all. Then, while Eoin did the final washing up, I went to lock in the cows for the night, first checking that no lame ones had stayed anywhere behind in the cubicle sheds. I found one or two of those all right and hushed them out. Then I noticed a shape in the darkest corner of the furthest cubicle shed. I was annoyed thinking that some right bitch of a cow couldn't walk out to the field but was able to find her way so far down there all right. It wasn't a cow at all , however, but 007.

Gingerly I made my way over to him. Still there wasn't a stir out of him. So, getting brave, I gave him a little tap on his rump and told him to get up out of that because his girls were long gone out and the young fellow would be having the fat and the lean of it. Then, however, he looked up at me with such beseeching eyes, as if to say 'You wouldn't — you just wouldn't, would you — make me go out with them all again?' I laughed out loud at the cut of him. And, still laughing, I went for Eoin to see this for himself. Eoin got the same imploring look, and, when he tried to shift 007 with a lot more force than I had utilised, it was still no use. Not an inch would 007 budge, not even when Eoin employed the prongs of a pike. 007 had had more than enough. He just was not going to go anywhere for anybody. So Eoin had to go for John-Boy, saying, as he patted 007 comfortingly on the neck.

'Poor old fellow — so you're getting past it too. Never mind: you'll feel a lot better in the morning after a good night's rest.'

Eoin then followed John-Boy and the lame cows out to the field. When he came in for his supper he informed us that he now had a name for that new bull at last. It seems that when John-Boy reached the field the young bull came up, locked horns with him, and it was the older bull who walked away. No way was the young fellow giving up the territory he had only so briefly ruled on his own. What he had he was going to hold at all costs — so he was named J.R. on the spot. But we will have to wait and see what kind of results our J.R. will bring — he may even be firing blanks for all we know. It does happen in the animal kingdom too you know!

Knocking His Own Share Out of Me (1982)

Aren't words funny things? In this house the same words or expressions mean quite different things to Eoin and myself than to our sons. I always think they are wrong and they think that I am quite funny — in their sense of the word.

At my present stage of life I can easily chart some of the changes in the meanings of words. I remember quite well, in my youth, when the word 'funny ' was in a transitional stage and we, as children, used to drive my mother mad when we'd always ask her if she meant, 'funny peculiar or funny ha-ha?' Now, to my sons it seems to be always 'funny peculiar' with their 'funny looks' and their 'funny house', which is where they'll drive me in the end. Their concept of funny and mine are quite different things, in every sense. Most of their so-called amusing stories would much better fit into their particular meaning of funny, being totally peculiar indeed. Yet, when I object they tell me not to get so 'thick'. Now to me 'thick' means stupid but they are thick enough, it seems, to consider it means getting unnecessarily cross.

The word change I most regret, however, is that of the word 'gay'. I've had to give up using it entirely when, one lovely summer morning, some years ago, I said that I felt positively gay and the boys, bursting into gales of uncontrollable laughter, teased me unmercifully then and for ages afterwards at the most awkward moments, about my change in sexual prefer- ence. And to think I was a married woman before I knew what the word homosexual meant! Now it is just a another subject for my sons' funny peculiar stories. This is such a pity, on two fronts. I dislike my sons telling off-colour stories in my presence. Also, there just is no proper substitute in the English language for the way I felt that morning as I whirled Eoin in a light hearted dance around the kitchen. Feeling happy is too static; cheerful, too forced; blissful or ecstatic, over the top; merry, possibly, except that now is also changing meaning. So, light-hearted is all I have left, and that, besides being twelve letters where three did the job so well, is not quite right either.

Generations have always reacted differently to things said anyway. What is considered normal once becomes no longer quite right as the years go by. When my fourth son, Pádraig, was born, Eoin and I met an old man, who said, as we went into Mass the next Sunday, 'I hear congratulations are in order again Missus. It must be a great feeling to know that you now have four fine sons to shoulder you to the grave....' Both Eoin and I thought that was a most peculiar thing to say by way of congratulation on the addition to our family of yet another boy. Yet, my mother, when I told her of my annoyance, didn't see it that way at all. 'Wasn't it just the plain truth he was speaking?' she countered. But I still was far from pleased to have such intimations of our mortality thrust on us just as we had taken on still more responsibilities.

Eoin and I aren't always so much on the one word though. Just a few days after this church door incident he was baling straw for a neighbour across the valley — in those days he did a lot of that kind of outside work to help with the finances. When the woman of the house brought him out a cup of tea in the field, after congratulating him on the new arrival she asked how many sons that made it now. 'Four, thank God' was Eoin's proud reply. 'Four is it?' said she nudging him in the ribs. 'Faith now, Eoin lad, but aren't you knocking your own share out of the little girl...?'

Eoin was in stitches telling me all that when he got home again. But I could see nothing funny at all about it, except, perhaps in the meaning those sons later take for normal. To tell you nothing but the truth I was extremely annoyed, and foolish enough to show it. So, for years afterwards, Eoin used to tease me about 'knocking his own share out of me', especially when the fifth son came along in jig time. Just to rise me he'd then also use the expression in much broader contexts than that old woman first meant. Poor woman, I took an ever stronger dislik to her. But then I was young and foolish, and perhaps, a trifle sensitive too about producing four babies in four years. When one is sensitive about any subject one is then inclined to lose one's sense of humour. Eoin, on the other hand felt nothing but pride, then and now, in the quick arrival of all his five sons.

He didn't have much understanding either of how a friend of mine felt recently. She, also of this parish, had a farming son married quite recently. All seemed well with her, even in the awkward first few weeks after the young pair came home from their honeymoon. She has always been full of praise for her new daughter-in-law. Still, I was with her, on the street, when another neighbour came by and accosted us. After the usual pleasantries had been passed he turned to my friend and said 'I met your replacement after Mass last Sunday ... and she seems a fine strong girl anyway....'

I thought this funny, but my friend's face blackened visibly, and she rapidly changed the subject. I know my day for daughters-in-law isn't that far away now so I wondered if all was as rosy at home as this mother-in-law had made it out to be. So I summoned up my sympathy for her when the neighbour had gone on. I am not so insensitive that I do not realise that it must be hard to be so summarily reminded that our place in life is, or at any rate can be, taken over by another. That fact is inevitable, and unpleasant.

Not having yet met the daughter-in-law in question I then wondered, to myself, precisely what was meant by a 'fine strong girl anyway'? Rumour has it that she didn't come empty-handed to the marriage. And I was reminded of a local wag, who, on seeing another new bride at Mass the Sunday after, said to his cronies at the chapel gates that the fortune must be great because the beauty wasn't much. That then was repeated ad nauseam and I only hope to God that it never came to the ears of that bride and groom .

Usually anyway, being told that one is fine and strong means that one is just plain fat. So I do not appreciate those remarks made to me how fine and strong I've got in recent years. I'm not sure that I appreciated the so-called compliment one girl paid me after a recent garden walk here either when she said that my ᵓuse had a lovely lived-in appearance. I have no doubt but that she really meant how untidy it was, and doubtless she is quite correct in that too. So that was why I was inclined to take umbrage.

Still, to leave that alone and get back to the question of replacements, I can't help but consider the care we take with our dairy replacements. We examine the breeding lines of both sire and dam and then their own conformation and appearance also is taken into account when we decide which calves we are going to keep to replace the cows that leave the herd each year for whatever reason. We try to always have those replacement animals a good deal better than those we cull out. And yet we now leave the choice of the other, more important human replacements to such a chance emotion as love.

It wasn't always the case however. I, myself, am the result of a made match, a match that worked very well indeed, especially for my father. In his case he got the beauty and the fortune combined. My mother, too, was very contented with her lot and never once, as far as we know anyway, considered remarriage after my father's death. Indeed, when I fell headlong in love she said to me, one day, that a made match was the same as putting a cold kettle on the hot stove of married intimacy — it quickly reached boiling point. But there was every danger in a love match, of an already boiling hot kettle being put on the cold stove of the harsh realities of married life without any money. She said that kettle quickly lost its heat for good.

Now I wonder when should I be on the look out for my likely replacements ... and if my brood will take any more notice of me than I did of my mother? I know, from experience, that a hot kettle on a stove that's constantly attended to through the years is the best solution of all. And no, I did not have a fortune to bring to Eoin....

Who to Dye For? (1983)

The other day a group of us stated to discuss age at one of my committee meetings. Someone there had commented that since we were all roughly of the same age did we really think that so-and-so and so-and-so would fit in well with the group? But what were we to do since both these women, one much too young and the other miles too old, in her opinion, had been both proposed and seconded at the last meeting.

Looking around me I could see that she was quite right, in one context anyway. There we all were, somewhere in our forties, be it early, middle or late, plus, of course, Peggy, who is determined to stay at forty nine for at least another year. That we were all much of a same age is proof, I think, that any existing committee strongly influences those who later join. I was never sure whether this happened wittingly, as in co-option, or unwittingly, with like always finding like. Then, someone commented that, except in the extreme cases in point, in fact it was now extremely difficult to tell the age of anybody since there we all were and not a grey hair to be seen amongst us and she, for one, would like to know when exactly a woman should stop colouring her hair.

There was a moment's absolute silence and some surreptitious sideways glances, with each of us sure no doubt that nobody had suspected our own 'dye' job. Yet I, for one, was well aware of the tell-tale grey parting, especially at the crown, when others were overdue a tint. Anyway, now it was all out in the open, the suggestions as to when to go grey then came fast and furious. These ranged from a decided 'never' to 'I suppose when my first grandchild comes along'. That came from a member none of whose children are even remotely near marriageable age as yet. 'At sixty,' said a woman in her late forties I'd guess. 'At fifty,' said another whose fortieth birthday was recently admitted.

'I'm going to stop colouring the hair on my head the day I find grey hairs elsewhere...!' said another hard case with such a ripe chuckle that we were left in no doubt precisely what she meant. When the laughter had died down someone asked if we all wouldn't have been better off if we had never started to cover over our grey hairs at all. Then we'd be spared a lot of time and expense, plus the need to cover our heads when the sun shone so as not to have the colour bleached out on us, or have the telltale foxy look when the sun shone through our hair. That advice is no doubt admirable, in hindsight. But it was already too late for all of us in the room.

I was more interested in the fact that all the women present seemed to consider going grey such a traumatic occurrence that it had to be linked to a significant occasion such as a milestone birthday or a major family event. Unfortunately, it may be that the major family event may, in the end, be a traumatic one, the death of a husband, when one just does not have the heart to continue the pretence of not having grey hairs any more. I know I've seen that happen more than once among my friends and acquaintances. This, of course, does beg the question of who do we dye for anyway — ourselves, our men folk, or everybody else in general. While it would be nice to say we really do it for our husbands, I know quite well I do it for the general public. Except for those of us in an outside job, in daily contact with others, there are few of us making weekly trips to the hairdresser for the regular touching up of our roots. For me, and many others I know, it's a case of getting a box from the chemist or supermarket and doing a quick dye job ourselves at home when we just can't face out any more as we are.

There is regular war in this house on that subject. 'Couldn't you have done that some other day, woman?' is Eoin's regular complaint when, once again, I decide to touch up my roots too late on the day we are going out somewhere. He scolds and scolds while I, having barely waited the necessary time for the colour to take, wish he'd leave me alone to get on with washing out the excess colour and go and do his shaving down in the kitchen. He still doesn't realise, after twenty five years, that it is only the spur of going out that makes me do it at all. He finds it hard always to accept my haphazard ways.

I get things done all right, but only at the very last minute when the real pressure is on. I seem to need that adrenaline rush. What I don't need is him fussing and fuming while I achieve miracles under pressure. Another of his major complaints is the way I always go house-cleaning when visitors are expected. 'It takes all the good out of it' he says. One day I must tell him that it also takes all the good out of it for me when he spends his time giving out to me instead of taking the duster or vacuum cleaner in hand himself. He, of course, is always dressed and ready miles too early for everything. If I didn't use deliberate delaying tactics he'd have me miles too early everywhere we go.

He is the sort, anyway, who must always put on a clean shirt and a tie before he goes out anywhere, even to the cattle mart. I have often heard him too, when he comes home, giving out yards about the cut of most farmers there. I have never known Eoin to leave this place, unshaven. So he finds it very hard to have sympathy for any man who doesn't run some sort of a razor over his face from Sunday to Sunday. He also swears that a lot of the farmers he meets only put on a clean shirt on a Sunday morning and that then has to do them, day and night, until the following Sunday morning, or so his nose tells him. And men's sense of smell has always been notoriously bad. I know I get the whiff of smelly socks occasionally when we are out socialising with fellow farmers, when Eoin only notices the clean shirt and smooth shave. I blush for the good name of farmers whenever such pongs hit my nose, because I fear that there are good grounds for thinking that farmers are a dirty lot, and not only because of the kind of work they do.

I fear there are possibly questionable grounds too for committees all being composed of like minded people. Our chairperson was instructed, when making out the list of committee candidates for our upcoming annual general meeting, to be sure to put the two women so objected to at the very bottom of the voting paper. Then, by a process of elimination, the rest of the names were ranked in the order of the present committee's preferences. There was no such nonsense as ranking people strictly alphabetically. The rank and file of the membership don't really care who goes on committees, it appears, just so long as they themselves escape. So, out of indifference, or indeed sheer laziness, they almost invariable make the choices from the top names on any list, sometimes not even bothering to read it through.

And so it came to pass at that annual general meeting. So the committee changes are merely cosmetic — like our hair colouring.

It's Not Good News (1994)

It is not good news here. We had our second herd test last week and failed. And it is not a case of a light outbreak of TB either. Of course to say that you have only a light outbreak of bovine TB is akin somewhat to saying that one is only a little bit pregnant.

One reactor, or fifty, equally locks one up indefinitely and causes endless upset and hardship. The number of reactors only measures the degree of financial hardship involved. Yesterday we had twenty reactors. So they are still here, still milking away, and it is heartbreaking to look at them, each with their death warrant signed. And, to make it worse some of them are safely in calf to AI. It is never the bad cow that reacts somehow. Our first serious attempt at upgrading the herd and now look at us. 'Why do we bother?' said Eoin in total disgust.

Our last breakdown was two years ago when we lost twenty-one fine cows. And it is only this year that our numbers are back up to match our quota. The extra replacement calves kept then calved down this autumn. I know the official theory behind the compensation money is that one goes out and replaces the lost animals with fresh stock once one goes clear. But by the time that happens the young stock could be nearly there and anyway we have never had great success with bought-in stock. Admittedly, the last cows we bought in had to face into the winter yards and severe competition from the rest of the herd. They lasted no battle and were all gone within two years. But the experts now tell us that new animals should be introduced to a herd only on grass. Otherwise, they are best kept separate until they hit grass. But life here is complicated enough as it is without running two herds in the one yard. Anyway, we have to have two clear tests first, sixty days apart before we can even contemplate such an action. Even if all goes well that will take us back into the autumn again. I don't know. I am beginning to agree with those who wonder why anybody bothers to improve and expand. Those who don't seem to get on all right and with a lot less fuss and worry too.

We knew quite well that we were gone down, the day before the official reading of the test, because the lumps were clearly visible on the cows as they came in for the evening milking. Anyway, what else could we expect with the neighbours still in trouble three tests after this latest breakdown in the area. Some were saying we were 'steeped' as it was staying clear this long. Now our herd has no contact whatsoever with any neighbouring herd but of course we have the same wildlife in common. Badgers are no respecters of boundary fences. We have a wood as a boundary on one side and I am sure that it is from there

they come. We have failed, however, to find evidence of fresh
sets there, so we are still theoretically law abiding citizens. But I
grit my teeth when I read that notice on local shop windows of
an association called Badger Watch and a list of phone numbers
to ring should anybody see any interference with badger earths.
Years ago badger hunters used to come on our land regularly
before we reclaimed it all. I never welcomed them then but I
certainly wish I had a contact number now.

It is amazing how circumstances affect your opinions. There is
an old saying that it is easy to sleep on another man's wound.
Well, it is also easy to protest and picket on what only affects
another man's pocket. I get so cross when I hear of the pickets
and protests about animal welfare by people who never had to
care for, or depend on the well-being of animals for their liveli-
hoods. We sent bullocks off to Egypt some weeks ago, fortunately
before we found ourselves locked up. Now, with all the commotion there was in the press at the time we did wonder what the
conditions on the boat were really like, as well as whether we
would have to run the gauntlet of a picket of protesters with our
lorry load of animals. 'Phone back for reinforcement troops if there
is the slightest sign of trouble,' Eoin Óg was told as he prepared
to follow the lorry. Getting his bullocks to pass the Egyptian
buyers was, however, the only barrier he faced at the docks.

While there, waiting for his animals to be inspected, Eoin Óg
asked to see around the boat, in order to see for himself the
conditions the animals would have to face. What he would have
done if they were really terrible is a question I did not inquire too
deeply into. But, in fact, he was quite pleasantly surprised. All the
animals were in reasonable sized pens, with two water points in
each pen. They were well bedded and had a huge supply of
excellent hay in front of them and for the voyage. Actually, it was
that amount of hay we heard most about when he came back,
since fodder was becoming kind of scarce here at the time. That
was the main reason after all this lot of bullocks were being sent
off to Egypt, to relieve the pressure on food stocks for the rest.
One pen in ten on the boat was empty. He was told this was so
that each pen could be emptied in rotation so that they could then
be thoroughly cleaned out during the voyage. Right in the middle
of the boat the smell of ammonia was a bit strong. When he

commenting on this, however, he was told that was because the fans did not work until the ship engines were started, and the ventilation system was both explained and shown to him.

'Was the dung just thrown overboard?' I enquired, but that was one question he had not asked. Anyway, even if it is, that cannot be anything like as bad as pumping untreated sewage straight into the sea. Eoin Óg finished up his description of his day by saying that he would far prefer to be a bullock on board that boat than a seaman. So when he gets depressed about losing all his pet cows, and they are pets with him, I will remind him that as bad and all as it is being a farmer with TB in one's herd he could have been a sailor with less room to himself than a bullock.

Who Have I? (1998)

This morning, hearing the voice of a somewhat neglectful son, talking to his father, I turned off the television, put away my knitting, took off my glasses, lay back in the bed and closed my eyes. In other words I settled into a sick old woman pose.

Then, while waiting, I remembered a relative I used to visit, years ago. Once I remember her son and I sitting on a garden seat, facing the house, talking for a while. It was a lovely day and I was loth to move even though I could see the person I had really come to visit looking out at us from her bedroom window.

'I'm glad to see your mother up and about again,' I commented idly. 'Last time I was here she was in bed and not at all well.'

'She'll be that again by the time you get indoors,' was his somewhat cryptic reply. Having seen that she was fully dressed at the window, I thought he was being a little hard on his poor old mother, who, incidentally, was younger then than I am now.

Anyway, when he took me upstairs to pay my duty visit, there his mother was, prone in the bed, wearing a white bed-jacket and the thick bedroom curtains were tightly drawn. Then, through the gloom, came this weak wavering voice: 'Who have I...?' Her son, pulling the curtains to let in the glorious sunshine once more, said, 'now you can see that for yourself, Granny!' and he went off about his business. Sitting by the bed I proceeded to fill her in on all the family news, including any juicy bits of local gossip. She soon perked herself up and her voice became fine and strong, and her laugh hearty, as I continued my visit. I pretended not to notice that underneath her bed-jacket she appeared to be fully dressed.

When I went home, I entertained Eoin with the full details, even mimicking that faint inquiry of 'who have I...,' to great effect. Today, decades later, those words came back to haunt me when I realised just what it was I was doing, getting ready to put my own son through a deliberate guilt trip.

That other day I thought the whole performance was put on for my benefit because it was months since I had last called. But maybe I was wrong. I have no way of knowing quite how long it was since her son had last been in for a proper chat. People say to me that I'm lucky having family so near that I need never be lonely. But it doesn't always work out that way. They have their own lives to lead and the days can run into weeks, unbeknownst to them whatever about me. However, while I have Eoin, I really don't need them no matter how much I might want them.

So there was no justification really for me to do my 'dying swan act' in the bed, just because I was feeling hard done by. If I had only thought a bit I would have realised that it was a waste of effort anyway: my generation is the last generation to be so easily manipulated by guilt. That is the crux of the problem, the suspicion that mine is the last caring generation. Even though, mostly, we now have nobody left for whom to care, those who do either have their old relatives living with them or else seem to have a set rota of duty visits. One friend goes to see her mother every Tuesday morning, without fail, and spends the whole morning with her.

'My mother can still tell by my voice when I'm lying,' she once said, explaining why it is easier for her to go and visit rather than phoning up making excuses. 'I'd feel too guilty anyway if I didn't go' she continued.

Another friend now visits an old aunt twice a week, ever since she went into a home, because she appears to be so very lonely there. My friend knows quite well she has made the burden for her own back by making her caring visits such regular occurrences. But I suspect that her real problem is a certain guilt that she did not take her aunt to live with her. In actual fact, however, that aunt of hers is extraordinarily difficult, short of temper, with a tongue as rough as a rasp. Yet my friend and her husband continue to visit her and it is not out of fear that the nursing home may refuse to keep her.

I know, from experience, that I couldn't do as they do. I too had an aunt like that, who lived to be ninety eight and grew more and more bitter with each year that passed. Yet my youngest sister continued to visit and care for her well-being right up to the end. There seems to be always someone who cares in every family despite all the rebuffs. My friends in question recently became grandparents once more, this time by a son in Australia. So, naturally enough, they went to visit immediately after the event. The aunt was duly told all of this and was so upset that they promised they wouldn't stay longer than two weeks even though it was such a long way to go. Being retired, they have all the time in the world to spend precisely as they wish. But stern duty prevailed and they turned down the opportunity to stay longer.

The day after their return they went to visit as promised. But, instead of being pleased, the aunt lit into them both. She tore strips off her niece, bringing up the past history of her mother. The tongue indeed can be a fearsome weapon. The nephew-in-law fared little better. He was also read, seed, breed and generation. Finally, in a fury, the old lady rang her bell for the nurse, issuing orders that they never were to be admitted again. I'd have left shaking the dust from my feet. But not my Christian friends. Three days later they went back, to be welcomed with open arms. So all is fine now until the next time they are less than attentive. Why, with all their own care flown the nest, have they taken in a cuckoo, voluntarily, from whom only death will free them if they continue to allow her to treat them like that?

How the old aunt manages this control, through ill-temper, is totally beyond me. My own aunt Kate was exactly the same. I swear my mother was afraid of her. After each duty visit she'd come away totally upset. Yet her conscience kept bringing her back, again and again, to do her duty by her dead husband's sister. That same woman had led her a merry dance always. She, an unmarried sister, supposedly caring for her father, was in the family home when my mother married my father. My mother's fortune then partially went to this sister I believe. But that wasn't enough for her. Some short time later, when my mother and father were away for a planned day out, they arrived back late to find Aunt Kate gone and my grandfather left on his own, confined to his bed as he was. So he could do nothing about the fact that not alone was Aunt Kate gone but so too was almost everything in the house that wasn't the personal property of my mother. It appears that the furniture removal vans arrived within an hour of my parents' departure and were loaded up with, firstly, items of value and then, with anything at all, while space allowed.

That was the last that was heard of Aunt Kate until a year or two later she sent for her letter of freedom since she was getting married in London, and the local parish priest spread the news, my parents only hearing it third hand. In fact I was nearly grown when the famous Aunt Kate finally came home, one Christmas, swathed in furs with a compliant husband to heel. Oh yes — she also brought with her the smallest box of chocolates imaginable for us children. Funny the things we remember. And, I knew nothing of the past family history then or for many a year later.

Now that she is dead and I grow older I do try to understand her mentality. She, and my friends' aunt grew up in times when, if they didn't marry or become nuns, they had no chance for self-fulfilment. Yet the potential was there for them to be great. My aunt was full forty five when she took off, with no training, and found both pensionable work and a well-to-do husband.

Maybe, since I am supposed to be the spitting image of my aunt Kate, I'd have been just as bitter if I hadn't met Eoin so early on. And, as due warning, I did also tell my friends that my aunt left everything she possessed to a religious order for Masses to be said for her soul. Nothing went to any child, deserving or not, of her only sister-in-law.

MAY

Elections Just Aren't the Same Any More (1981)

Elections just ain't what they used to be. I was amused at the boys' reaction this week to Eoin telling them some of the tales of the elections of his youth, not to mind those of a still earlier generation who thought nothing of travelling miles and miles to the huge political meetings in the earlier part of this century. Eoin's father was involved in one famous one where de Valera came to Cork, in a motor car, to address such a meeting. On the outskirts of the city, however, de Valera got out of the car to mount the waiting horse. Black cloak swirling about his long lean frame, he then rode in state through the crowd to mount the steps up to the platform. He, or his handlers, surely knew how to work a crowd.

Feelings really did run high in those times. My family were of a different persuasion from Eoin's, and they must not have been as politically involved as the Kavanaghs either because I have no memories of anything to do with elections. I was married before I got my first chance to vote, so that may have had something to do with it. I was also married before I heard ditties like Eoin sometimes sings around election times — he still toes the family line. I have one ditty in my head at the moment which is driving me distracted, because I can't get beyond the first few lines, and neither can he. So maybe somebody can tell me what comes after:

Some say the devil is dead, the devil is dead, the devil is dead
And buried in Killarney.
More say he rose again, rose again, rose again
And joined the Free State Army.

As far as I can see, if my own are anything to go by, the young people today hardly know their own political affiliations not to mind those of their friends or family. Now, whether this is a good thing, or not, I have still to make up my mind. Listening to Eoin's tales of his youth and the bad feelings that arose, between good neighbours and friends, as elections neared, makes me wonder. I am amused that the jeers and taunts that passed between them then were of an even earlier generation. 'You're only one of the shoot, loot and scoot brigade...,' was the favourite catch call around here with the 'die-hard' families, to throw at those whose families once favoured the Free State.

Eoin must still be strongly of the belief that the fault all lay on the other side as he told of his neighbour, Denis, a good friend in normal times, who, when elections loomed, would pointedly hop over the ditch so that he wouldn't have to talk to Eoin, simply because their respective families voted on opposite sides. A week or too after the results were known, win or lose, this mad notion would have worn off Denis and he'd go out of his way to meet up with Eoin once more, even if it meant this time hopping over their boundary fence to have a chat in the middle of their work.

It wasn't always that peaceful, however. Eoin was with his uncle, whose first name he bears, when they came home from Mass, one Sunday, to find his uncle's house daubed with paint and slogans of all sorts. The 'shoot, loot and scoot' one had pride of place on the hall door. Even the dog had been given his ration of paint as had the uncle's neat evergreen hedge, the pride of his life. He was the kind of gardener, Eoin said, who, while he was eating his meals, if he saw as much as a stone in a flower bed would have to go out and remove it. And as for that beautiful hedge, Eoin was there, he told us, when that was newly planted and when, during supper, his uncle saw a rabbit nibbling at one young tree. On the spot, his uncle left the table, got his gun, and discharged both barrels at the rabbit. The rabbit scampered away, but his uncle had blown the tops off the whole line of young trees, as neat as you ever saw. Eoin said that they were lucky that, in his rage, he hadn't turned the gun on himself. But both barrels were empty.

The sons were more interested in the damage done at that election time, however, especially when Eoin left it slip that the perpetrators don't live a million miles away from us today.

'Who was it Dad?' they clamoured, all agog with curiosity. No way would Eoin tell, however, despite their best entreaties, and rightly so too. I already knew anyway. Still there is absolutely no point in either opening old wounds or starting any trouble into the third generation. So Eoin changed to the stories of the time he spent driving a party car the day of elections. It was his own car, needless to mention, but he put it, and himself, at the disposal of the party ferrying people back and forth on all election days. He thoroughly enjoyed himself, getting the vote out, he told us, striving to be first to each house without transport. The whole idea was that which ever side brought them to the polling station then had the best chance of getting their Number One when the passengers went into the privacy of the polling booth.

Now there was this one particular man, a little bit simple all right, but cute with it. He was the one who used to always give to the end of January, with his wren bush, traversing the length and breath of this and adjoining parishes. He, and not others, was best able to take advantage of his simplicity. Anyway, on one polling day, Eoin and other party cars called on Johnny to go voting. But Johnny gave them all the same story. No way was he going to budge until seven o'clock that evening, for any one of them. My ever over-punctual Eoin was there precisely at five to seven. While he was waiting for Johnny to put on his cap and coat, however, another car, with two men of the opposing party, drove into the yard. They waylaid Johnny as he came out his door and endeavoured to show him the error of his ways, telling him all their candidates could do for him and saying, 'never mind that die-hard, Johnny — come on with us and we'll buy you a pint afterwards....'

They then, however, made the mistake of each taking Johnny by an arm and attempting to frog-march him into their car. Johnny, never the most patient of men, broke free, rushed over to the dung heap and, grabbing a four-prong pike, made for his tormentors. They quickly made for the safety of their car. An enraged Johnny kept on coming however, and, despite a futile attempt made by the driver to parry his thrust with the car door, the dung pike went through that door like a hot knife through butter. Eoin laughed at the memory of the moment and the shocked expressions on the faces of his rivals as they stared unbelievingly at the pike quivering in the door of their fine car as Johnny strolled with a self-satisfied air to Eoin's second-hand Austin.

The last laugh, however, was on Eoin. When he got to the polling station, very much the victor with his passenger, Johnny got out, and, in his usual loud fool's voice, put on when he was being at his most devious, said 'Youse can all go and f*** yourselves now — I'm not going in there at all at all...' Then, to the great amusement of all the onlookers, he stalked off down to the pub on his own. People never just went to the polls to vote, then. The men spent ages hanging around, both before and after exercising their franchise, waiting for any diversion, just as they did at the chapel gates, before and after Mass. So Eoin's discomfiture was well noted and discussed. It took him forever to live it down as it was trotted out, election after election, for years to come.

Yet, regardless of such slight blips, Eoin enjoys his elections, then and now. His sons, however, can't wait for this election to be over. Television addicts, they are sick to death of all party political broadcasts. The thought of no television at all while the great vote counting fest continues, is, for them, the last straw. Their father, however, is already metaphorically girding his loins for the marathon. Therefore, they haven't even the faintest chance of turning over to the other channel. I swear Eoin enjoys the count as much as a race meeting, with the various party tipsters extolling the certainty of their dead certs. He keeps track, with pen and paper, of the figures for the different counts and guesses where the surpluses will flow, listening to the commentators pontificate and the experts' obtuse explanations. Finally, he even enjoys the official reading out of the results, in varying tones and accents, some hilariously incongruous, especially if the experts have been proven wrong. Eoin, anyway, is of the firm belief that the tally men are the only ones worth listening to seriously.

If, by any chance, I do sit down with him for the night's count, which is unlikely since the boys already have half-wrung a promise out of me to take them to the pictures that night, I will enjoy, not the count, but Eoin enjoying the count. This, however, will not keep me from my bed, although his side stays cold as long as there are any results possibly still to come from the 'box'. The fact, however, that he stays up late to watch television results isn't much of a story to tell future generation of election fever in the 1980s, now is it?

Asparagus and Strawberries (1996)

Today Eoin and I lunched off asparagus and fresh strawberries. Sounds awful grand doesn't it, when put like that. But, whatever about that, it tasted damn nice and was all the nicer because I had grown the lot myself and it hadn't cost us a penny beyond our time. And, with my way of cooking asparagus, I wasted no time over a hot stove either.

I can never understand why so few people grow this most delicate of vegetables when it is the easiest thing in the world to do. And, once a big bed of it is established, you have it for a lifetime. It just gets better and better as the years go by. Just what is a big enough bed is the only problem I've encountered with asparagus since I have just extended mine once again. That was because I discovered, last year, that asparagus, micro-waved, is truly finger-licking good. Thus, our demand for this vegetable has increased yet again. Before, steamed or boiled, I found it nice, but not really nice enough to rave about. I was happy instead to sell it at the country market for what seemed to me to be vastly inflated prices.

Now, having first cut off the end of each stalk until the knife goes through like butter, I lay the spears on a plate with a lump of real butter on top. Sprinkled with sea salt and covered over with cling-film, it then goes in the microwave. And never again will I cook it any other way, since it really is a meal on a plate, the butter, salt and juices combining for a gourmet meal in literally minutes. Mine takes seven minutes per pound of aspara-gus, but microwave ovens vary of course.

The real secret is that it is fresh from the garden. As for it not costing a penny, this is because I grew the original lot from seed, and have since saved seed the odd year. I carefully space the seed in seed trays in the spring and there they stay until the following year, when they have formed good root systems and are big enough to handle easily. The original ones I planted out in what was really a waste bit of ground which I had sprayed really clean of perennial weeds, and given lots of strawy dung. I also, then, gave each plant a good two foot square, simply so as to fill the full area with the plants I had. That, I think, has been a major, if accidental, part of my success with asparagus growing, and has led to really fat succulent spears. Everywhere else I have seen asparagus growing, even in the most stately of homes and gardens, the plants are really crowded together and, since they are capable of forming a root system of at least two foot square, such overcrowding must stunt the plants.

How I am running on about the growing of asparagus? Eoin, except when he is eating the results, often swears at my gardening enthusiasms. Still, this year, at long last, I think he may well have caught the gardening bug. But not from me. I know quite well that I had little enough to do with the gratifying sight of him walking around the garden, dead heading and weeding, with a bucket in hand. Indeed I am beginning to think that I have a serious rival for Eoin's affections in Helen Dillon, since he so looks forward to seeing her on the Garden Show. He hangs on her every word just to hear what she is going to come out with next. Then, if I have missed the television programme, I hear precisely what Helen has said, or recommended to be done. This week it was 'that brute of a weed', the fast seeding little bitter cress, that Helen had Eoin chasing, in among the flowers and in the gravel beds. And, just as she recommended, the lot went into the bucket. Before this, the times I was lucky enough that he did any weeding at all for me, it was just a case of throwing the weeds further back into the flower beds, there to wilt where they landed, spreading their seeds still further. The question I now want to ask is how come Jerry Daly never fired Eoin's enthusiasm the way Helen does? But I have also heard of husbands being jealous of Jerry Daly from time to time.

Still, all jokes apart, I am only delighted that Eoin is starting to take a serious interest in the garden. It is a great hobby for a semi-retired farmer. And, just as farming programmes once, watching gardening programmes on television now has been very instrumental in firing his enthusiasm. Actually seeing the results, and well as exactly how to achieve it, does make it all seem possible somehow. Gardening programmes are prescriptive as well as descriptive, something that no longer really can be said of farming programs on television. Does anybody else remember Telefís na Feirme, with presenter Justin Keating, which really set about teaching us our trade?

Farm walks were another way we learnt our trade in the early days, a most pleasurable activity. Actually, that is what I think Eoin likes so much about the gardening programmes on television, the fact that he can visit all sorts of gardens from the comfort of his own armchair. Perhaps, shortly, he will be ready, willing and able to take on garden walks here himself. Now that would be something. It is that time of the year, anyway, when the notion to go garden-walking hits people. This week I got two requests from groups to come and see my garden.

'Did you say no?' was the first question Eoin asked when I told him. So much for his being willing! But of course I didn't say no. I'm much too flattered that anybody would want to come and see my garden to say no. Anyway, it is so beautiful these bright May mornings that I am only dying to show it off. I swear my own family don't even see it as they pass through on their way somewhere else. So it would be nice to hear 'well-done' whether my garden visitors mean it or not.

'Big School' (1995)

Michaella started national school yesterday and I was a lot more tearful about that fact than were either of her parents or indeed the young lady herself. She couldn't wait for the day to start 'big school'. It has been a count down for the past two weeks with her nursery school days drawing to a close. And, of course, it meant buying her a school bag and a pencil case and all of that. It seems only yesterday that we sent her father off to the same school with a school bag almost as big as himself. That was what made me that little bit tearful I think, the passing of the generations and the wondering did we do everything right for our sons. Would he have been better off if we had waited another year to push him out into the big bad world? With hindsight, I think that an extra year or two going through the school process is a good thing. I had sons doing their Leaving Certs at sixteen and barely seventeen, and all because they started national school at a very young age, and not because they were exceptionally bright.

They all started national school when they were just four, or in Pádraig's case before he was four at all, since the custom then was to start school after the Easter holidays the year the child was four and Pádraig wasn't four until August. I have a cine film of that momentous day in his life, but I feel quite sad when I look at it. He had three older brothers and he desperately tagged along after them in the playground and the older one, Michael, who had been warned to look after him, pointedly ignored him. But two little girls took him by the hand into school when the teachers arrived. It is all there on our silent bit of film. No words need to be spoken, anyway, to know exactly what was going on. I feel the tears rise, because, once they start going to national school, in a way they are gone. Pádraig, my frail one, took his first steps away from me when he walked through the school door that day. I see him dragging back and looking over his shoulder at me, his mother, who was allowing all this to happen.

Actually, it is a lovely bit of film because all the children were quite unconscious of my presence there with the camera as they played in the school yard. Other mothers were also there with their first day mites. Now, that cine-camera of ours, which we bought to register our joy in our first born, has recorded every bit of our children's growth, from their coming out from the maternity hospital to adulthood. I remember that I thought it quite a luxury at the time, it cost eleven pounds, but Eoin was mad to have it. The film was relatively expensive as well and each reel only lasted four minutes. So this made us record only the big occasions. Nowadays, I see everybody with their easy-to-manage camcorders and cheap video tapes. Then, it was something troublesome, and expensive. Pádraig and Sara do not record anything like enough of the big occasions in their daughters' lives, however. I keep telling them it's something they will regret when their children grow up. Isn't it odd how, if something in life comes easy, people just don't seem to bother? It never occurred to them, for instance, to bring their camcorder to have Michaella's first day at school on tape for ever more, to share with us all since it is an occasion that can never be repeated. I would have loved to have seen her in action, and she, when she has children of her own, would also greatly value that record.

Her mother told me that, once again history repeated itself when some of the bigger girls came and took charge of the newcomers and Michaella happily went off with them ignoring her mother as she opened up her school bag to show off all her prized new possessions, chattering away quite unselfconsciously. Michaella made me laugh when, calling in here on her way home that first day, she said that there were children crying a lot but 'they were only babies'. There was also some big story about butterflies as she ran around me flapping her arms in the air but I did not quite understand what that was all about. She is quite self confident, my little missy, and why wouldn't she be and everybody loving her to bits since the day she was born. She is not shy. But then she has had the benefit of play school two or three mornings a week, for the last two years, and it shows. Like all children she needed other children to play with and to get used to sharing as well as learning. There she is now starting off national school and she can count, do simple sums, and knows all her alphabet if her song from Sesame Street is not interrupted. So, she has a great head start on the children who have not been to playschool. Of course that does not make the slightest difference in the long term but it is yet a further boost to her self confidence now.

If I was her fairy godmother self confidence is the one gift that I would like to give my much loved granddaughter. A self confident person appears to glide through life and attracts friends easily regardless of beauty or brains. In my generation girls' self confidence was whittled away quite deliberately by parents and teachers. 'Don't be making a holy show of yourself' was dinned into us from a very early age as we were trained to sit quietly, to speak only when spoken to, and not appear to be precocious with minds of our own. I hated my teachers and national school days with a hatred which still simmers in my heart to this day. But my sons have none of that resentment and, if her first day is anything to go by, neither will Michaella ever be consumed by such venomous hatred because of the damage done to one as a child.

Gardening is a Disease (1994)

Gardening is a disease. Make no mistake about that before you take it on. And it is a progressive disease too in that it only gets worse. And, on top of all that, I personally am torn between two lovers. My garden is demanding so much attention right now. But I also have much too much college work, not to mind all my own MA deadlines, and I just can't be in two places at once.

Then, last week, Eoin came to find me one day. And when he did finally run me to earth, in my plastic tunnel, he was quite cross, and wet. 'I've been looking all over the place for you Liz!' he said, with the emphasis on the Liz. 'Oh oh,' I thought, because Eoin never calls me by name to my face unless he is really cross with me. Otherwise it is just 'love', 'sweetheart', or such. Or, half absentmindedly, at times he calls me Mother, something I do not really like at all. I am not his mother. Also my sons only call me mother when they are cross with me. 'Oh Mother!' speaks volumes in my family.

Anyway, in my plastic house poor Eoin promptly walked on the edge of a seed tray and the crack of broken plastic went through me. Quickly getting off that he stepped backwards onto a row of little seedlings in pots, and finally came safely to rest in the narrow pathway which is all I have left uncovered now up the middle of my tunnel. 'Only that you have no room left you'd have your so and so bed over in this place too and then I'd never see you at all,' Eoin added crossly, pointedly ignoring the damage he'd done. Then, in damage limitation, he added 'And anyway what on earth are you going to do with all these plants. You'll finish up simply giving the half of them away.'

Of course he was quite right. I had just spent hours, having escaped the books, very happily potting on tray after tray of seedlings for no other good reason but they were there. Last year was such a fine summer that all sorts of seeds ripened beautifully. Then, this year, in February and March I sowed dozens and dozens of different lots. I love sowing seeds. And every year, as well as my home saved ones, I also try quite a few new bought packs. As always everything I do I do to excess. But seeds of most of the annuals are so easy to save, sweet pea, snapdragons, asters, lavatera and such, that I can afford to be prodigal. Actually, with ones like love-in-the-mist, and the opium poppy, I just go around the garden, sometime about now, with my half buckets of seed, and just throw it around the place, in any potential bare spaces. Some of it doesn't germinate, more of it comes up quite in the wrong place and has to be weeded out again, but the rest makes a great show in the summer time.

Of course not everybody would agree with my kind of gardening, which is to fill up every available or semi-available spot and not to worry overmuch about heights or colour schemes. Formal garden schemes go well with grand houses or in town gardens. But in the countryside, personally lacking the Georgian-type house, I prefer the simpler cottage garden approach, a mass of colour most of the year around, not an inch of bare earth ever to be seen, as though Nature herself had done the job.

Actually some of my most successful effects are indeed self sown. At the moment, in my new gravel beds, surrounding the car turning area, there are violas run riot, which I grew from seed last year. I did not have many seeds to the packet, and my new gravel beds needed planting up, so they were spread thinly about. The result is that, each single plant has this year sowed itself for yards around, so I have a sea of blues, in one area, yellow in another, purple over further and so on. The effect would never have been so good if the colours had been mixed.

So basically that is what I try to achieve in my garden, great swathes of plants, repeated over and over, to give a unified impression. At the moment I am digging up clumps of daffodils, those now too close to expanding trees or shrubs, dividing them up and sticking them in to any area where the daffodils are a little scarce right now. Whether they are in bloom or not doesn't really bother me, or them. This means too that there are great patches of the same variety then close together, in what is now a bare area, when my divided clumps really thicken up. This seems to work better, gives a more natural self sown look, than all the varieties every second one so to speak.

My gravel beds in front of the house, really only came about because the gravel was supporting so many self sown plants, that I just sprayed off some of the lawn and covered it with gravel, to deliberately continue the effect. Then I decided, last year too, that the same should also work in the tunnel. The big problem with plastic tunnels is that, in such ideal growing conditions, weeds grow even faster than the plants. So there I first covered the floor area with plastic. And God knows there is plenty waste plastic lying about this place. Then I covered everywhere with a thick layer of fine walk gravel. The pots, of all sizes, just stood on the gravel and looked extremely well, especially when I covered the potting compost in the pots with some of the same gravel. But, most importantly, hardly a weed grew all year, either around the pots or in them.

Now the gravel is supporting dozens and dozens of seed trays and I am truly happy tinkering about there half the night. But Eoin is not. What was it I said about being torn between two lovers? I better revise that upwards to three. And next week my two granddaughters are coming to stay....

College is Over — Now What? (1995)

I am thinking that college is like a toothache, great when it stops. From today on I should have time again for my garden and my grandchildren. My exams are over, the last one being the last day of May. My four years are done. I should have letters after my name in July. Liz Kavanagh BA has a fine ring to it, don't you think, even if it is a bit late in the day for it? But was it all really worth it? That was the question being asked in the pub after the last exam when tongues were loosened by the strain of it all being over, as well as by the drink. Everybody there said, 'yes, but....'

There were only two known love affairs among us in all the four years, and neither was licit. So those who went to college with such hopes failed, and it appeared that some had indeed started out with that in mind. Most of the younger people, and a lot of the older women are unmarried. But there was a decided shortage of older eligible males. There was even one young man in English, who, whenever a girl got talking to him, waved his shiny new wedding ring around a lot to display his ineligibility. Of course the young girls soon twigged this and deliberately engaged him in conversation just to see the performance.

Now when I talk about older here I mean over thirty because we fell into three broad age categories, the young, the middle aged and the wrinklies who were there for the sheer love of it. The young, of whom many were unemployed, were trying to get third level education for which they did not qualify on leaving school. Quite a few of this age category got married over the period, but to people they knew beforehand. Most of the middle group were gainfully employed, but wanted to better themselves in their careers. And this is something that surprised me greatly, the advantages there are to be working for some companies more than others. The civil servants got all their fees paid, and a month's paid study leave as well, plus two days off for each exam. The ESB and Bord Telecom also had good arrangements in place, as did the main Banks and the Gardaí. The Local Authorities are not quite so good, just so many days for each exam. But private companies, such as the insurance companies, gave no allowances whatsoever, for their employees. Their exam time came out of their annual holidays. The message came across loud and clear that the young should pay a lot more attention to all available perks when they start work, and not just the initial starting salary.

But the young among us said of course that chance would be a fine thing, that there just isn't any choice these days. Some of my classmates, however, both young and middle aged, have already got choices to make. All of those I was talking to any-way, who had applied for to do their H.Dip. had already been offered a place on the strength of their performance ever before the final exams. Others were given provisional places dependent on gaining a certain mark in their finals, which of course was dependent on how the current crop of day students did. There are about four people looking for every H.Dip. place I am told. In a way it is tough on the day students doing their finals the same year as the night class do theirs, because it means that there is all that more competition for scarce H.Dip. and MA places. Personally, I would wonder about the future of anybody hoping to get into teaching with the falling birth rate and all of that. But that is what these students are determined to do. Some of the married women, with children they cannot really leave, said that they will then be qualified to give grinds in their own homes, which is the best paying job of the lot, straight into the back pocket and all that. They have no notion of school teaching no matter how well they do next year.

I then told them how they could give grinds without the

credentials if they had the neck enough for it. You see, one night in the college restaurant, the young girl opposite me, with pride told her companions how she was in the money big time. It transpired that the week before she had been in her local shop where somebody called Anne Marie BA H.Dip. had advertised to give grinds in English and French, had left a blank sheet of paper for prospective pupils to write down their telephone numbers. So what did my lassie do but take down that sheet of paper, and ring up the list of telephone numbers saying that Anne Marie was no longer available but had asked her to take on all her students. And she was in business, with eleven pupils already and not one of the parents had asked her qualifications for the job. So none of them knew she was only a second year student of English and French. I would dearly love to know how those pupils got on in their Leaving Cert. I questioned her ethics in my own mind, apparently fully occupied with my meal and not eavesdropping as I was. Her friends, and some of mine, however, all seemed to think she was dead right. She saw an opportunity and took it, and that was the end of the story as far as they were concerned. And, doubtless the Anne Marie, who had put up the original notice, gave neither her second name nor her phone number, for reasons it is not too hard to guess. More back pocket work no doubt. Maybe she got her just deserts, pipped to the post as she was.

So what will the motley bunch of us soon to be graduates do now. We fervently vowed to keep in touch, but that was the drink talking as much as anything else. But it would be interesting to see what happens next to us all over the coming years and see what, if any, use we make of the hard won letters after our names.

Silage Cutting Now and Then (1997)

This week the silage was cut, harvested and sealed down, in double quick time. It was never faster. Once again Eoin Óg has changed contractors and I must admit that each time I am staggered at the improvement in gear, and the ground covered in the time. I am also staggered at the cost of the machinery owned by just one man.

I was passing up the yard, to help Eoin get in last year's colt foal for the vet to do a little job on him, when I heard all these voices coming from a tractor temporarily parked there. It was obviously not a radio station. It sounded much more like a group of lads having high jinks. So, of course, I proceeded to investigate. Then I discovered that each of the tractors is fitted with a private radio system. So, what I was overhearing was the conversation between all the drivers. And no, I won't embarrass them by revealing what I overheard in my snooping!

But, afterwards it was explained to me that the whole idea is that the tractors drawing home the silage can communicate with each other so that the outgoing tractors do not meet up with the incoming ones on any narrow piece of the road. Anyone in trouble can also call immediately for help and not have to go looking for a phone, or walking back to base. Mechanical help was never far away anyway, since it appears that one of the tipping trailers does more than just tip out its silage load. The whole base rises and underneath is a full tool shop, gas welder and all, to do all repairs on the spot. Also I never saw trailers the size of these. Each one took between thirteen and fourteen tonnes per load so they were no time at all clearing out our silage crop, even from the fields at a distance.

The harvester had no bother at all keeping up with all eight trailers, gobbling up at least twelve acres an hour as it did. And it looked as if it could cope with even more at its ease. It was some sight. Actually, our silage field was like a race meeting that night, as many came specially to see this latest in silage gear. I hate even to think of the value of the equipment, but I was told, by one of the callers, that you'd get a farm of land, plus appropriate milk quota, for the money invested in all this silage gear. They, therefore, just have to get through the world and all of cutting each day, to survive the repayments.

So, bigger and better is the order of the day in all facets of farming, whether it be co-op mergers, increasing farm size, or the silage contracting business. Grow or go. It is as simple as that. Loyalty no longer comes into any equation with the modern young farmer. And who is to say they are wrong. Our generation

were much more inclined to stick to the devil we knew in prefer-
ence to the one we didn't. We felt safer that way, in more ways
than one. We knew the neighbour would always be around
when the stranger was gone.

But isn't that the exact same argument used about the small
neighbourhood shops when the supermarkets came in? And it
was the small shops that went. People go for value for money
any day of the week, regardless. I see the sons hammering out
their deals of so much an acre and weighing that up with the
time each contractor is likely to be at the job. That is where these
big outfits score. There may be more men to feed for one meal.
But that is a much easier proposition than having less men, but
for a lot more meals. That was the one thing that used to drive
me absolutely wild, all those men coming in to be fed, even
when no silage was coming into the pits because of break-
downs.

Ah well. That is all history now. Eoin and I have seen silage
making change from the mower and buckrake, to what happened
here this week. Come to think of it, when we first started making
silage, almost forty years ago, there were no silage contractors
at all on the job, nor for many a year afterwards. The next step
above the buckrake bringing in the grass, straight from the field,
was the side attached forage harvester, which had to be unhitched
and left, each time the load was full. Those harvesters, no
doubt, will eventually finish up in farm museums, along with
the horse drawn hay-floats of my childhood.

What fun we used to have on those as the big cock of hay was
winched on board. Then came the long ride home, in front, where
one had to behave, or at the back, out of sight, where there was
freedom. My sons, as children, had many the ride home too, in
the comfortably full, single silage trailer, of that first forage
harvester. But my grandchildren cannot be left next nor near the
silage making these days. The modern farmyard is no place for
children, with no little jobs for them to do. So, is it any wonder
that so many of them, when they are growing up, would nearly
get lost if they strayed too far from their own back door. They are
not brought up to see farming as the natural path to follow. And
therein lies the seeds of much of the flight from the land, in
second place only to that need to get bigger and bigger to survive.

The next step in our silage making getting more mechanised was when we co-operated with a neighbour, who also had started making silage. Job specialisation arose as each of us took on specific tasks and machines. Silage making literally then went on for weeks on end, as the compliment had to be returned in full, as in the times of the threshings in my own youth. But neighbours, these days, no longer seem to co-operate. The days of the meitheal are well gone, replaced by hard cash negotiations. And, as one who remembers the threshings and hay making of old, the quality of life for the farming women has improved dramatically over this period. My daughter-in-law has life far easier than I did, just as I had a far easier life than my own mother. And Eoin Óg's life is definitely made easier by the sheer speed with which the silage was safely gathered in, this week, in perfect weather, with a trailer load to the acre. Now that that's all done, my young pair are talking of heading off for a week's holiday next Sunday, with the relief service taking over.

Personally I think they are mad, leaving Ireland at the very best time of the year, and Eoin's eyebrows were raised a little too! But could it be that both of us are just as envious as hell?

JUNE

The Womb-less Club of Ireland (1980)

'Welcome to the womb-less club of Ireland,' read the card with
the first lot of flowers delivered on Monday morning. And, in
spite of my stitches, I had to laugh. I wouldn't doubt my friend
Helen. She always had a great sense of humour. She did not lose
that with her uterus, five years ago now.

I had emergency surgery early on Sunday morning and,
when I woke up again, I was told I'd had a hysterectomy but I
was doing fine. Eoin was there beside me, all concern. But,
honestly, I was so far out of it that I really did not care. I hadn't
cared either when, the night before, the doctor Eoin had insisted
on calling, had me moved straight into hospital. Eoin said that
when I just lay there in the bed, and would neither talk nor
read, he knew something was desperately wrong.

I'd had a miscarriage on the Friday before, with the usual D & C
done that afternoon. Then, after an overnight in a corridor in
the hospital, I was glad enough to get home again even though I
felt really wretchedly ill. This was my no means my first miscarriage or D & C. So I knew what I was talking about when I
told my gynaecologist that I really was having the most dreadful pains. But he as good as pooh-poohed the idea that anything
could be wrong.

So, like a good woman I shut up and went home. But, once
there, I just crawled into my bed wanting nothing more than to
be left alone. Thankfully Eoin did not accept this, however. So,
at ten o'clock that night, he brought a strange doctor in to me
because our own GP was away for the weekend. He had earlier

tried to get my gynaecologist on the phone only to find he was gone, that day, on a two week holiday. So that may have been why he was so anxious to send me home out of the way.

'Don't you ever give me a fright like that again,' Eoin said to me as he held my hand tightly. The surgeon had just told him that I had a severe form of blood poisoning, which could have proved fatal. Eoin, of course, asked how this could have happened, under hospital conditions, but he, closing ranks, said something about incomplete miscarriages, and my age.

So my entry to the womb-less club was a little unexpected to say the least of it. My fellow club members in the ward had had plenty of time to prepare. And, since the word went out of what had happened to me, Eoin has been overwhelmed with the advice and information given to him. All of it has been very well meaning, no doubt, but I am only grateful to those who went out of their way to cheer and encourage him. He needed that to counteract some of the old wives' tales told to him in all seriousness.

He was assured that, when I got out of hospital again, that I'd be impossibly moody, depressed and tearful. If he could put up with that, however, then in about five years' time he would have some semblance of his old Liz back. But I'd never be quite the same, ever again.

That same day I had my own Job's comforter when one of my visitors (whose husband's sister's cousin-in-law had a hysterectomy and so she knew all about it) told me that, of course, I now would have to be prepared for an immediate menopause — with all its rigours. These she outlined for me in full detail with much whispering and head shaking. In spite of myself I found myself getting more and more depressed.

I was a captive audience in the bed anyway. And soon she had drawn in the rest of the ward into the conversation. Each had their own mite of mis-information to add. Where they got it all was totally beyond me. One even knew of a woman who had produced a baby a full twelve months after a hysterectomy. Now that I could scoff at. But, if I did, she immediately dived into her locker and produced a women's magazine with just such a freak case in banner headlines. This then did the rounds.

When my visitor finally left, as our tea was being brought in, I was totally depressed, so much so that when Eoin came in that night he soon had the whole story out of me. It was then that I learned about all the tales of doom and gloom which had also come his way. Mere acquaintances, he said, had taken pleasure in telling him to expect the worst. Yet he was only laughing at the good of it because he had been already been forewarned by Helen, the sender of my flowers.

She, and another post-hysterectomy member, had put Eoin straight when he delivered his sons, who were cashing in on my absence, down to the Country Market. After the checking in, they told him that they now felt better than they ever had before. They also warned him of all the scare stories he'd probably hear. He was to take no notice of them, they advised, and, above all, he was to make sure I took no notice of them either.

There would be, they assured him, neither side-effects nor after-effects apart from me having to take it easy for a month or two. Then, he could look out because I'd then be flying faster than ever. 'So take no notice of know-alls who know nothing' Eoin finished his pep talk to me and I was perfectly happy again.

Isn't the power of suggestion frightening? When I was expecting to feel depressed that's exactly how I felt. Then, when convinced of the nonsense of that, I immediately cheered up again. But next morning I still asked my surgeon, when he called on his rounds, which stories were true.

He, poor man, with a sigh, and eyes-up-to-heaven-heard-it-all-before expression, sat down on my bed for a chat explaining just why there could be no truth to all those old wives tales since my ovaries were still intact.

'You could say, Mrs Kavanagh, that I've just taken away the pram but left the play-pen intact,' he finished up and even the hovering nun cracked a smile. So, any of you facing a hysterectomy you can take it from me that, apart from the first week or so, there is nothing to it. And it does have one very useful side effect.

Every woman should be seriously ill about once every five years. It frightens one's family into a due appreciation.

The Harem in Ward Five (1980)

These past weeks I've discovered a little of what it must be like to be living in a harem since practically all the women in Ward Five seem to be violently in love with their doctors whether they realise it or not. Some do verbalise their feelings all right, telling us how kind, how marvellous, how gorgeous their doctor is. I've even heard how they love his clean white shirts and his brand of aftershave. I know this is a welcome change from cow-dung for some of us, but antiseptic is surely a more fitting smell for a doctor going from patient to patient on the morning rounds. They tell of how clever he is with his hands and that they know for a fact the number of lives he has saved. But I find myself wondering if my surgeon washes his hands between patients?

He, since I first was his patient aged twenty-two, always calls me 'Honey', possibly because he can't remember my name, and his hand is inclined to fall, ever so casually, on my breast, as he talks to me. I know I should object, and have in the past, but in a peculiar way I enjoy it this time.

I bet you never knew that the surgeons and especially the gynaecologists of Ireland were such brilliant and handsome men — not a female doctor comes near Ward Five anyway. And I wonder do their wives know of all the heart-throbbing they cause as they do their daily ward rounds? They are the lucky husbands indeed if those wives put half as much effort into attracting their attention as I see going on all around me here.

The pots and jars start rattling with one patient shortly after the six o'clock morning temperature round. While the rest of us sink back into a deeper sleep her beautification commences and the transformation is complete by the time the rest of us surface, pale and frumpish, for breakfast. But there she is, lying back on her pillows, primped and painted, hair becomingly curled and wearing yet another peek-a-boo nightie.

The first morning I noticed this, I commented to the others (when she had gone to the loo of course) how marvellous she was to take such pains so very early in the morning. 'Ah, but her doctor comes in early' came the cryptic reply from the bed next to me. And sure enough, after her quick trip to the loo the lipstick was touched up and the neckline of her nightdress readjusted a few times with frequent glances into her hand-mirror.

When quite a lot was displayed my neighbour winked at me, knowingly. So I, too, eagerly awaited the appearance of this Adonis, the cause of all these preparations. I even put on some lipstick myself because you never know.... Alas, shortly after, what came in to her was this small, balding man, with a positive paunch and pop-eyed to boot.

'How are we today? And 'good, good,' he said, without waiting for a reply. Then he bounced out again while she looked at him like a lovelorn schoolgirl. Once the door shut behind him she visibly relaxed and presently fell asleep. When she woke up she was perfectly normal again, joining in the chat with the rest of us and ignoring her cosmetic box. Next morning, however, the whole performance was repeated, and has been, every morning since, except Sunday.

Yet the funniest one of all happened here today. We had a new patient in yesterday who went up for her hysterectomy this morning. She seemed to be a quiet, mousy enough woman, and, as her gynaecologist comes in already to another woman in the ward she didn't even bring the interest of a new doctor with her. She did not contribute much either in soul-baring over-night, so we did not take too much notice when she kept her curtains pulled and her radio on while waiting for the trolley to wheel her away to theatre.

The nurse had been to give the usual pre-operation injection an hour or so earlier. We, therefore, presumed that she was relaxing in her own way listening to Gaybo on the radio. Then in came the trolley and the attendant nurse pulling back the curtains said 'Come on now Mrs Murphy we're all ... great God above.' We all sat up at the note of consternation in the nurse's voice and looked at the vision the drawn curtains had revealed. Talk about a filmstar! Peach negligée matched the masses of peach make-up. Finger and toenails were a bright vermilion as were her lips.

All hell was let loose as the nurse, no longer cheerful, called for help and a bevy of them started in on a scrub job with flannel, soap and nail varnish remover. Rubbing at the gold eye-shadow removed eyelashes and all. No wonder her eyes were so spectacular with those yard-long false eyelashes.

The biggest struggle, however, was to get her false teeth out of her mouth. But leave them after her she had to, top and bottom, and it was a very different creature who was wheeled out finally with the nurse still muttering crossly. Of course it is the nurse who'd get the blame if the theatre was delayed waiting for her to arrive. But no way could the patient have been taken up as she was. We all had a good laugh, when she was gone, in spite of our stitches, at the length Mrs Murphy had gone for the benefit of her gynaecologist.

I couldn't wait to tell Eoin all about it when he came in later on. I never once told him, however, about 'Honey' with the wandering hands. He might not believe me if I said that was good for my recovery, the realisation that I wasn't completely unsexed by my hysterectomy. But I do seriously wonder what makes all women patients crave for extra attention from their doctors when they are under their care.

PST *and* PMT (1994)

It has been a rough week here and yet it also has been an excellent week because we managed finally to get all the silage cut and the crops were absolutely tremendous. When Eoin Óg and Lisa left on their honeymoon, after their incredibly wet wedding day, we joked about us leaving the covering of the silage pits for them on their return. While this is indeed a most unpopular job here, we little dreamed how much rain would fall since they left and how very nearly true that threat turned out to be. Eoin, since his accident, is also out of things.

Between the jigs and the reels we only finished covering the pits on Saturday and the honeymoon pair flew in on Sunday night. But they are spending the first night or two with Lisa's parents so have not reported for work just yet. We, of course, met them at the airport and they are looking marvellous, all bronzed and relaxed, which is more than they found any of us.

Tell me, does everybody else find silage making quite as stressful as we do here? You know we used always joke to Eoin about women suffering from PMT once every month, but he only suffers from PST (pre-silage tension) two or three times a year. Now, with the advent of the menopause I have finally got rid of my PMT. But, does anybody have a permanent cure for PST? And please don't say retire from farming, because this week proved that would only work for Eoin if we moved house as well.

Poor Eoin was out of all the silage action with his leg so injured by that bullock, but he wasn't out of the house. And I swear his PST was worse than it has ever been before and that's saying something. Poor Pádraig was the one doing all the running. I was the one doing all the cooking. Eoin, however, was the one doing all the suffering. He is supposed to be still in the bed. With the help of his crutches, however, he made his way around upstairs to lean out the different windows to try to see the fields they were picking up, or at least hear the noises of the silage trailers coming and going, and also see how the pits were being filled. I got a call in the midst of washing a mountain of spuds to go and find Pádraig to tell him that they were not leaving the yard pit out far enough to start with, that they would find themselves drawing in too fast now at the top as a result.

'Nobody but myself knows what to do there,' Eoin complained bitterly. 'And if I'm not after their arses all the time it won't be done right!'

I'm not quite sure whose were all the arses that he had to be after, but I think that both his son and his wife were included with the silage men. He had also given me full instructions about just how many dinners were to be taken out so as not to delay the work. I had the idea that to have everybody come into the kitchen at the one time would simplify my work. But Eoin always took the meals out to the man mowing and the man on the silage harvester so as to keep those working, while I fed all the rest in the kitchen. So, that was the way it should be done, and no other way would do him, just as with the correct filling of the pits. Then Eoin started to worry about the effluent drain not being constantly checked to make sure it hadn't been accidentally blocked with grass, now that he himself wasn't able to personally oversee that as well.

But of course everything was going perfectly. Pádraig was playing a blinder, as he had to, with both his father and his brother missing. There was the usual quota of breaks and punctures with the silage gear all right, but sure such things are normal. Eoin's biggest worry never happened. That is that the forage harvester would find and swallow something in one of the silage fields that shouldn't be there, like a bit of a concrete block, an iron bar, parts of machinery or whatever. You know yourself the kind of stuff that goes out with the dung or the slurry in the winter time and is never picked up when it should be. You also know what can happen if, perhaps while fencing, something like an iron bar is carelessly left behind. That is the only explanation there can be, surely, when such things go missing.

The damage done to the innards of the harvester when such things are swallowed doesn't bear thinking about. Many years ago we were sued by a contractor over just such a happening. After that we used to religiously walk all of the silage fields every spring to pick up all the deleterious matter from stones to bits of plastic. But somehow, the sons don't appear to do that any more. And every silage day Eoin swears that next year they will have to begin to do that again, whether they like it or not, and then that will be one worry less on his own shoulders. Poor darling, he worries not only about every thing that has happened to us in the past but also about all that may happen in the future.

But at least we never had a tractor stolen during silage making. On one farm we know, when the silage men came out after their dinner, a tractor had completely disappeared from where it had been left in the yard. There was great commotion, naturally enough. The guards were called in and I even believe that the details of the tractor were broadcast on Garda Patrol. However, neither sight nor sound of that tractor was found. The insurance money was duly collected and a new tractor bought. And, by the autumn, all concerned had as good as forgotten about the stolen tractor. Then, when the same contractors were in that farm to empty the slurry pits late that autumn, half way

through the yard pit their industrial loader hit something hard
in the slurry and was unable to shift it. So they gradually worked
their way around the obstruction, and yes, you guessed right,
what they finally uncovered in the slurry was the missing tractor.

At least nothing quite like that has happened here this week,
despite Eoin not being in charge and Eoin Óg being away.

'Hooring and Touring' (1994)

Well, poor old Odie's hooring and touring days are finally over.
This week he was taken to the vet and decommissioned. And he
still is not talking to Sara because she was the one who took him
there. But then she is also the one who has to put up with him.
And she does have two children now to more than keep her
busy, fond and all as she has been of that dog. The only trouble
is that Odie thinks he is a human male, I swear, and that she is
there only to look after him. Pádraig got him as a pup as a
present for her, his bride-to-be, but presented him to me, his
mother, to rear despite my swearing that after the sons and their
dogs I would never again have a dog in my house.

Honestly the difference it makes having the dogs in the yard
and not in the house is incredible. I don't care how clean a dog
is, there is always that doggy smell, dog hairs all over the place,
and fleas, especially in the Summer time. My sons used to
regularly take their dogs to bed with them when they were
young. Then, calling them in the mornings for school, I'd often
see two little heads, theirs and the dog's, on the pillow.

So, of course, I also had a regular flea hunt, turning over the
blankets one by one searching both sides for those shiny black
spots. This would always be after I'd see those tell-tale red rings
with their central brighter red spot on my sons. Then, the cap-
turing of the culprits and the squashing of them between the
two thumb nails without them escaping, was a skill in itself. I
remember reading once that children under four were immune,
or so it appeared, to Rocky Mountain fever. This was what
eventually alerted doctors there to the fact that fleas were the
carriers of that particular disease, not by their bite, but by their

blood: children under four do not have the co-ordination necessary to kill fleas in the time honoured manner.

Do people get bitten by fleas anymore? I can't tell when I last
saw those give away little red circles on anybody. Yet I remember a most embarrassing moment for me in the maternity hospital the day Pádraig was born. His was a daytime dash, because
Eoin was particularly busy cutting silage with a neighbour, so I
put off the moment of going as long as possible. Then, when I
was safely delivered into the hospital, and Eoin, as normal, had
gone back home to the other boys, I put on the new nightie for
the public viewing that went with childbirth.

As I undressed, however, I was horrified to find several flea
bites on my thighs. There was no mistaking those red rings. So
what was I to do? There was no way to get rid of them, such
things only slowly faded. So, in between the labour pains, I
scratched hard at those marks until they bled. At least then they
looked totally different. Next, to be sure to be sure, before the
nurse came back with the razor for that embarrassing shaving, I
grabbed my dressing gown and rushed out to the bathroom
where, with the help of the small mirror of my powder com-
pact, and the totally inadequate mirror over the sink, I searched
my back for any more flea marks.

Of course a few hours later, and Pádraig was a bad breech
birth, I couldn't care less about any marks on my body. When all
was over the self-inflicted scratches still remained, however, to
the mystification of the nurses. One said I looked as if I had been
through a briar patch backwards and what had happened to me?
I said nothing. As soon as I was home again, however, I searched
every bed in the house for fleas, and I found the culprits too.

But fleas are only part of why I do not want dogs, especially
pups in the house. Pups destroy everything. Odie ate two pairs
of Eoin's slippers, the original and the replacement pair. And
each time it was the right foot was chewed up so that Eoin
could not have even a odd pair to wear. It was only when we
left the utility room to Eoin Óg and his bride that I finally threw
out those two perfect, but useless, left slippers. Which action I
soon regretted since that pair's child substitute, their bitch
Grover, collected the day after they arrived home from their
honeymoon, chewed up the left slipper of the current pair. So

once more I had to go shopping. Did you ever notice how children never repair the damage they do to your things, but woe betide you if you don't make everything right for them?

Still, to get back to Odie and his emasculation, he would go through hell and high water after any bitch in heat for miles around. The times he came back in a pitiful state, after being chewed up by a local large Alsatian, who staked a more powerful claim to any bitch, never taught him a lesson. But the Alsatian and his owner left the area and Odie, growing in prestige and aggressiveness among the neighbouring dogs, regularly disappeared and then came back, exhausted but physically unharmed. He always came back in the middle of the night, however, and noisily demanded to be left in. He would keep on barking until either Pádraig or Sara got up out of their warm bed and came downstairs to let him in. More fools they. I always said that he should be chained up outside and never be in the house anyway. And there are laws about having dogs always under control. But that is the trouble with the first dog every young couple have. I wasn't joking when I said they are child substitutes.

Which is fine until the children come along and that need is fulfilled by the real thing and not the substitute. So, getting up in the middle of the night to a new baby is bad enough, But, being disturbed when she had just got back to sleep again after the two o'clock feed by a randy dog coming home to comfort after a night out, was more than Sara could stand. So he was threatened, warned, locked up, and still he escaped one night too many. So that is why he was decommissioned this week. Which will be a relief, no doubt, even to himself, eventually.

But is there any cure for a pup which insists on digging holes in the garden? And it is no use saying keep it out of my garden. I did tell you that it is a child substitute for Lisa and Eoin Óg. But hopefully that situation will change some day too in due course.

Women's Place (1997)

Sometimes, when I listen to 'experts' I wonder if I am living in the real world at all. I was at a talk during the week about the place of Irish women in society and there is no way that I recognised myself in what was being said there about farm women. Women's work on the farm was called unpaid work for the farm owner. So the inference was, in a patriarchal society, farm wives are either victims or fools.

Sometimes I despair of so-called feminists. Personally speaking I have never felt myself to be either a victim, or a fool, because Eoin and I have always run this place as a joint endeavour. What money there is belongs to us both and we share it. I can write cheques just as well as he. There has never been a question of his taking out money for his own personal use before it became generally available to us as a unit. Indeed, I know quite well too that in the past thirty odd years I have had considerable influence both on how we ran the farm, and how we spent our money. The concept of my work feeding calves, or doing anything else either, as being unpaid, I consider a total nonsense. Payment to me for farm work would be just a transference of money from one pocket to another with no gain or loss to either Eoin or myself.

But after that talk I have been doing a little extra inquiring, and, indeed, listening. The listening bit has been most informative because some women talk in the same terms as I do, about 'we' and 'ours'. Most women, however, seem to say 'he' or 'his', especially those who work outside the farm, or who never set foot much in their own farmyards. That specific use of pronouns, I think, speaks volumes about where the real control lies. Only a widow spoke in terms of 'I' and 'mine'. But then again not all of the men I spoke to used 'us' and 'ours' even though their wives did. So am I part of a dying breed of farm women, having always being so involved in the day to day running of this place, and making sure our sons did their fair share of farm work too? Could this be part of the reason two of them are farming now?

Women have a much stronger effect on farming structures than is generally realised by men. For many decades Irish women, especially from the smaller farms of the West, have demonstrated their feelings about farming by leaving rural areas in their droves and thus avoiding marriage to farmers, They have made a vote of 'no confidence' literally with their feet. By 1990 almost a third of all Irish farmers were unmarried. Here, in our parish, without ranging too far, I can count quite a few bachelors who would want to be hurrying up in the marriage stakes, or else they will find themselves permanently in that category.

Education has always been the most used avenue of escape from farming for girls, with mothers trying to enhance their daughters' occupational and marriage prospects outside rural areas, as a form of rebellion against the powerlessness of their own lives as farmers' wives. Studies here, and in France, have shown that even on the smallest of farms, the educational achievements of farm children far surpass those of any equivalent income group. Education has also been found to be the mother's domain. She is the one who normally puts extraordinary energy into ensuring scholastic success, driving children to schools and grinds and driving them on to work at their lessons at home. Fathers tend to put the needs of the farm above the needs of schooling. If a job has to be done on the farm then lessons tend to take second place. But since education is the domain of the mothers the fathers do not usually prevail.

The farm is a family enterprise whose main purpose is the establishment of the next generation. So, great effort is expended by the parents in farm work until the next generation is satisfactorily established, whether on or off the farm. Only then does farm work contract in scope and/or intensity. An heir settled on the farm, with a smooth transition of power, only that will prevent this inevitable scaling down of farm enterprises.

Intense commitment to education for sons as well as daughters, is a more modern phenomenon than education for girls, and is associated with rebellion against farming itself, and not just gender roles. Both parents may be involved here. They just want all their children out of farming, even though they may never have consciously formulated this desire. Alternatively, there may be a recognition that, while liking farm work, that pluriactivity, or off-farm work, is necessary for the survival of that particular farm.

So the net result of all of this is that however powerless farm wives may be in terms of control over property, labour or capital, children on farms, as elsewhere, as the feminists say, are 'the

inalienable right of women'. Since children provide the next
generation of farm labour, this careful cultivation of withdrawal
on the part of disillusioned women has important implications
for the continuity of family farming as a social form. Future
farmers, as well as the labour force for existing farms, is going
into higher education as much as into off farm jobs.

All in all the continuity of farm families is now more in jeop-
ardy than ever before in the history of farming in Ireland. I have
only to look around me to see that this is only too true. We are
in for drastic changes in rural Ireland come the new millennium
when all that is quietly happening, now, in the nineties, comes
to bear fruit. You mark my words.

JULY

A Farmer's Foot is the Best Manure (1983)

There is no doubt but the longer I live the more I understand and appreciate those who went before me. This week I even found myself remembering my long dead grandfather and one of his favourite sayings. Now, that grandfather of mine was never noted for his hard physical work. Indeed, I don't think I ever saw him putting a hand to either shovel or cow. Yet he used to be forever on the go, from place to place, so that his workmen never knew when or from where the Boss might appear. He was for ever humming a little song to himself, diddle-de-di music as he called it, while he walked around his fields and farmyard. I well remember him telling me, as I walked beside him while on holidays there, that a farmer's foot is the best manure. This didn't make a great deal of sense to me then. But this week didn't I find myself acting exactly like my grandfather and suddenly all was made clear.

Eoin was away for a few days, on a farming trip with his discussion group, so the running of the place rested fairly and squarely on my shoulders. The first morning, when it was past time for the tractors to be running and yet there was no sound, I was out up the yard, hot-foot. And there they all were, sons and workman, having a fine old chat while holding up the shed wall. Instead of lighting into them, however, instinctively almost, I backed away, unobserved.

Then I went forward again, but this time singing away merrily. Extraordinary to relate, as I rounded the corner this time, just seconds later, one was getting up on the tractor, another was disappearing into the milking parlour and a shovel had come miraculously into the third one's hands and he had started to scrape the yard. So all were at their allotted tasks. This ploy worked so very well that my musical repertoire has been well used ever since.

Now I understand just how my grandfather got the work done while avoiding confrontation completely. He had one big advantage over me, however. He was playing with hired help and not with sons. I don't know about you but I find it so easy to tell a workman what to do against telling a son what must be done — and why. And then, the crunch, why he and not one of his brothers must be the one to do it. Later still comes my quietly checking if he has done the job at all.

I keep saying it's the age group and that they'll grow out of it. I've used this 'age-group' excuse much too often these past five years, for everything from pimples to mood swings, from seemingly lack of interest in the job they are at, to downright insolence if they are left get away with it. I know they are much better than they used to be. But sometimes I do wish that those who tell us how lucky we are to have two sons working with us had the job of organising them for work. I have begun to thoroughly detest the sound of 'But what's he doing Mom?', which seemingly greets my every work allocation. I never heard them being that bad with Eoin. So, perhaps it's me, their mother, a woman, that they so resent being active about the place. But if I didn't keep after them the work would not be done properly and that's for sure.

They weren't best pleased with me today, when, on my rounds, I noticed an in-calf heifer with summer mastitis, calves needing moving on to a fresh paddock and cows really milling around a water trough so something had to be wrong there. My grandfather had been dead right when he said that the farmer's foot is the best manure of all. All the others on the place must have seen those things too at some time during the day. But the clues seemingly hadn't registered with them.

One animal standing apart from the rest, with her head hanging, extra flies bussing about her, always merits further investigation. And, of course, I know only too well, from sad experience, the prevalence of summer mastitis at this time of the year. A swollen udder, with heifers just beginning to develop, is easily missed, especially at a distance. I know, once summer mastitis hits, that quarter is gone for good. But, untreated, death is a likely scenario, which is far worse than a cow with three quarters. Anyway, we find that losing a quarter does not mean that a quarter of their potential yield is gone. We have quite a few three teat cows which far out-yield their four teat sisters.

The cows milling around the water tank should have called for closer inspection as well. One son admitted he had noticed that all right, but then thought no more about it once he had checked that it was full and the pump had not been switched off inadvertently or anything like that. Neither had they thought to do more than count the calves that day, to check that all were there. What they should have noticed was that the grass was very tightly grazed between the dung patches and the calves should have been moved on before they were forced to graze those, with their heavy burden of parasites from older stock. It never ceases to amaze me how Nature builds in safety techniques into even the way animals graze a field.

Of course my noticing eye has only come about with time and hard knocks. We have lost heifers to summer mastitis not noticed in time. Calves have not thrived and even died because of impossibly high parasite worm counts. But today's episode with the water tank was something I personally had never seen before. The water was there. Yet the cows at the evening milking were absolutely frantic for water and the level in the bulk tank was decidedly down. Because they were in the next door paddock after milking, using the same water tank which is under the electric fence, I had to insist that Eoin Óg go over after milking to find out if they were drinking this time. He was a long time gone but came back cock-a-hoop. The cows were on with the same antics, obviously wanting water but not going for it. Finally, in desperation, Eoin Óg put his hand into the water, to toss some out at them, doubtless in temper. But if he did he got a fine electric shock for himself. Then he discovered that somehow or another a loose wire from the fence was dipping, ever so slightly, against the iron of the side of the tank. That was all that was needed, of course, to give the poor cows a shock every time they went for a drink. So, even though maddened with thirst and plenty of water available, they had nothing to drink all this mad hot day. It was no wonder their milk yield suffered badly. Still, it would have been even worse by the morning milking if we hadn't found the answer.

I know quite well that without my getting cross the lads would all have been off for the night all problems at home forgotten. The stockman's eye, that ability for things that are not quite right to register, only comes with experience and, above all, interest. Suffering from my imposition of authority on sons all day I wondered if I had left total responsibility to them, with Eoin away, would this have added more to both their experience and interest. However, with sons, we are always in the old Catch-22 situation. We just cannot afford to give them total responsibility for running things until they have more experience, with so many of us depending on the daily milk in the bulk tank. But how are they to get experience without responsibility?

Eoin and I met a father recently, whose son was just back from a year in New Zealand, and to hear that man rave about the improvement in his son was quite something. He went to New Zealand, on a scholarship after a year in agricultural college and a year at home, when things were not good. But then he came back, as he father said, both fit, willing and able to take over. 'Not that I gave him the whole thing on a plate', continued the father. 'But I did give him complete control of the cows, on a percentage profit basis, as he suggested, and it is working out marvellously.'

It was obvious to me that the balance of power had shifted during the son's year away. It would never otherwise have changed, barring death or disaster. The young man had proven to himself, and his father, that he could manage farms successfully, because that was what he had spent the year doing in New Zealand. At home he had only been trained to be a good worker, a much easier task than training someone to be a good manager. I really must discuss with Eoin, when he gets back from his few days, the possibility of our lads leaving home for a while. I'm afraid that they didn't take the slightest notice of me today when I was telling them of their great-grandfather and his maxim of the farmer's foot being the best manure.

Yes Nos and No Nos (1984)

Do all families have special expressions like we do, the sort that are meaningless to outsiders. And it is only when you use it in someone else's hearing that you realise its strangeness. By no means do I include in such expressions the catch phrases that are imported by various sons over the years. Fortunately these usually die a quick death through over-use.

Michael, our Dublin son brought back the saying of 'get up the yard' and also, for a period, everything was 'stop the lights' from the television programme, *Quicksilver*, no doubt. Other sayings he brought home had to be put down with a really firm hand. When they started adding on 'that's what she said to me last night too!' to the most innocent remarks, the resulting lewd or hilarious results depended on your point of view. After a very few days we had to totally ban its use at mealtimes when even comments like 'I've enough now' or 'more please' brought on paroxysms of laughter. Eoin got very mad at times, mainly I think, because he usually did not get the gist of the joke, due to his deafness. He thought they were just being stupidly giddy.

You can only go so far in controlling that age group with their peculiar sense of humour. They think they are being so very daring. But sure, God love them, we have all been down that path ourselves in adolescence. There are very few of those kind of jokes we haven't heard before but have now, most of us anyway, thankfully outgrown. I have no objection to a blue joke, with a clever punch line that I don't see coming a mile off. But I do hate those people, men usually, who never outgrew their adolescence period, still trying for shock effect.

The kind of expressions that I mean evolve in family living and survive because of their sheer usefulness. We, here, have the 'no nos and the yes nos'. Indeed we had those in fact always but only in words these last few years. It was only put into words by me the night that I asked Eoin would he like a rasher and egg, or what, for his supper.

'A boiled egg will do me fine,' was his somewhat plaintive answer to me, up to my elbows frying rashers and stuff for the rest of them. It was easy to know from his tone of voice that he really would like a good fry-up but didn't want to put me to the additional trouble. So I proceeded to cook his lot next, ignoring the sons who were still looking for more rashers and sausages, French toast and/or fried potatoes. They, seeing the frying pans filling up again, because with my crowd I always have to have two frying pans on the go, began bagging what they wanted from each. I, however, insisted that their father be fed first.

'But didn't Dad just say no to you?' they pointed out with some justification.

'Ah, but that was a yes no, not a no no' I replied, guarding my frying pans. Eoin, at the table, had retreated behind the newspaper while all this was going on. But I was right. It did prove to be a yes no and he quickly demolished every last bit of his fry, as good as the rest of them, and with never a comment either.

The sons remembered it though. And from that night on they played on it. We are constantly being asked, to this very day, if it was a yes no or a no no when they ask to borrow the car or they offer us a bit of their chocolate, or whatever. They learned the lesson that night how so many of us often said no when we really mean yes. If a child is eating a bar of chocolate and offers you a bit, you won't deprive them of it even though your mouth may be watering at the thought of it.

We also say 'no, that's all right love', when the sons offer help, simply because we don't want to put them to any trouble. Still, I know that I really expect them to tell by my tone of voice, that I'd really love their help. The same sons, however, found out, to their advantage, that Eoin was inclined to weaken further when they ask him if that was really a yes no. They learned, like me, to distinguish the ambivalence in his voice. At other times the no would be so decisive that it wouldn't even occur to them to push their luck even the least little bit. Indeed, they now read the tone of voice so well that they rarely indeed ask if it a no no unless they are pretty sure it is a yes no. But if anybody was listening to all this going on, they would think all the Kavanaghs were completely off their rockers.

Yet, it isn't only within families that the 'yes nos' are employed. Indeed it used to be an old custom that, in order not to appear too grasping or anxious, you always waited to be asked the second time, whether it was for food and drink, or even marriage. Many years ago, at a threshing at my old home, when I was still young and impatient, my mother sent me around with the big aluminium teapot to offer the men, having their tea out around the threshing machine, a second cup of tea. Refusal followed refusal and I kept moving on down the line of tired dusty men, until my skirt was sharply tugged from behind and an irate voice said

'I thought you'd at least have the manners to ask me a second time....' And I was then instructed to: 'Sphill a sup in there now,' as he held up his empty mug to me. I had to retrace all my steps as empty mug after empty mug was then held up despite them all just after telling me that really they didn't want any more tea. That was how I learned to say, for ever more, 'Ah go on, do have another cup of tea', as part of the necessary ritual when going around with food and drink. The family say I still do it to them at each and every meal time and it is most annoying....

Now, in this context, there is one little thing that is bothering me at the moment. Our Country market AGM is coming up soon and I was asked by the outgoing chairperson, on behalf of the committee, if I would go forward as the new president at the meeting. I said no. But I am by no means sure, even yet, whether I meant a 'no no' or a 'no yes' to this request to be the head boss woman. Even more importantly I am not at all sure did she take my refusal as a 'no no' or a 'yes no'? That matters to me quite a lot.

Is there a woman or man alive, in Ireland, who ever said yes straight off when asked to take a leading position in any organisation? We all badly need the reassurance of being asked for the second time. But if that second request is not forthcoming , I must get to work to figure out what is the modern day equivalent of that tug at my skirt long ago. Now that they yet haven't had 'the manners' to ask me a second time I now realises, perhaps too late, that it really was a yes no I meant when I was asked to be the new president of our Country Market.

The Latest Child Substitute (1993)

With all the recent commotion about our TB reactors I never told you about the new arrival here. No, not that kind, no news on that front as yet, give them time. What arrived was the pup, the child substitute. With most newlyweds the pup usually comes first anyway. I myself got a beautiful red setter, Maeve, the nicest dog I've ever had. But for this pair it had to be a male golden retriever ever since they went to a dog show last year and there located the dog of their dreams. So, there and then they put in their order and once back from their honeymoon they went to inspect the last official litter that dog had sired. Then they came home and told us.

To say we were less than enchanted was to put it mildly. I know only too well the desperate damage a pup does, chewing on everything, animate and inanimate. And what it does not spoil with its front it soils with its behind. The stains left by the last child substitute in this house, Odie, who actually arrived before the honeymoon that time, are still here in the bedroom and living room carpets. He always went into a corner to per-form. Then I even had to take to walking about in my stocking feet so that I would discover the wet patches in time to take action. Odie also set upon, and destroyed, shoes and slippers of Eoin's. He also demolished a mobile phone which had been left, not by us but by his 'Daddy' Pádraig, on the couch. I had to give up putting anything out to dry on the line unless he was safely locked up first. Then I was regularly castigated for being cruel, and nothing about the fact that he destroyed every pair of tights I ever wore while he was a pup. He also dug ferocious holes in the garden. His 'Mommy' was a working mother then of course so the poor old Granny was responsible for that child substitute all day long. And enough is enough.

So I quickly made it clear that I did not care how many pups they got just so long that we had nothing at all to do with any-one of them. We did not want to know and said that anyway the only proper place for a dog was out in the yard. 'Why must you always be so negative, Mom?' said my son. My daughter-in-law said nothing but I was left in no doubt, by her face, that I had offended once again. Still I had a valid point. None of the dam-age done by Odie had ever been repaired, except by us, and I made the mistake of telling them this. 'Any damage done will be our problem' said Eoin Óg, as if his just saying so should be enough for me. 'Yes', I answered, the zip on my lip not yet fully

operational, 'Like the damage done that time Lisa's parents
were away and you brought their dog out here to stay. Tell me
who fixed that?'

Anyway, in the fullness of time the litter was weaned and
inspected quite a few times before they were fit to wean. Their
choice was collected one night and next morning it was brought
for our inspection. Well, we were allowed to look at him anyway, a lovely little white butter ball of a pup. So I made all the
right noises, admired it greatly as it nestled in Lisa's arms,
patted its head and left it at that, grateful that it had not disturbed us the night before, looking for its mother. You know
what pups can be like when first weaned. Then I was told that
he had a basket all prepared for him with a blanket and an
alarm clock. The ticking is supposed to comfort pups. But he
didn't spend much time in the basket. Grover, for so he was
officially named in his accompanying papers, had spent the
night in the connubial couch, or so my son somewhat ruefully
told me. And every time I saw it over the next few days it was
either asleep or being cuddled. Anytime it made its way towards
me, with the curiosity of pups, it was quickly retrieved. The
maternal and paternal instinct was mighty strong it seemed
about their 'lovely little man'.

Then the breeder of the dog was on the phone looking for
them. In their absence I answered it to find she had a little bit of
a problem. The litter was of five dogs and two bitches and she
was a bitch short when it came down to the last two pups. So
the search was on for the missing bitch. I passed on the word.
'Not at all' said my pair, when they were asked to check the sex
of their little man. So they phoned back and she went off to do
some more ringing around of her customers. But two days later
she was back on again, and again the following day, to ask them
if they were sure they were sure. But they were in doubt at all
and laughed at the idea of her making a mistake somewhere
when she had first checked the sexes of her litter of pups.

But a week or two later, the newness of possession having
worn off somewhat, Grover made his way unnoticed to our side
of the house. Now I swore that I would have nothing whatsoever to do with their dog, that I dislike dogs about a house. Still
and all, when it looked up at me with its sweet little white face

and those big brown eyes, I bent over to pick it up and cuddle it a bit. Lisa arrived at the same moment in pursuit of her darling. And I'll never forget the way her face dropped a mile because the very first thing I noticed when I picked up the pup was that it was a bitch. Well you can't really miss that sort of thing now can you? But they had. Now there is some excuse for Lisa. She is a city girl after all. But what about my fine son. As one of his friends said 'I'd be careful to check for myself the sex of any calf that fellow might sell me in the future.'

Others are promising him anatomy lessons before his first child is born, and one even asked Eoin if he had given his son that little talk at all before the wedding? Pádraig then chipped in to say that he is still waiting for 'his little talk'. He seems to have got on quite well without it. And I should know. Not alone is the proof positive there in Michaella, but there was also that awful day, when he was late coming back to work after dinner and Eoin sent me over for him because they were waiting for the jeep as well as him to get a cow to the factory in time. Well I knocked when I went over, the front door was open and Odie came out to meet me. There was no reply so I walked right in and disturbed them, hard at it, on the floor in front of the fire. I can tell you I was the one who was most embarrassed.

I beat a hasty retreat and when asked, on my return to the yard, where the hell Pádraig was with the jeep, I said I didn't know and disappeared again. I decided Pádraig could make any excuse he liked when he finally got over. No way was I going to open my mouth on what must have been the most embarrassing moment of my entire life.

An Appreciative Word Does Wonders (1997)

'You must always listen to thunder,' is a favourite saying of Eoin's and I am never one hundred percent sure what he means by this. Well, twice this week I think that I too heard echoes of thunder, so I suppose I must listen too.

First of all I met a retired school teacher, a much esteemed man, and in the general conversation that night he said that he had just the one big regret after all his years teaching. 'What is it?' said I, half expecting some big revelation: he was very much of the era of the 'bata mór' after all. I was taken aback, however, when he said it was that he had never praised his pupils enough. That was the one big regret of his life, that he should have given more help, more words of encouragement in general to his pupils.

'It might have made all the difference if every so often I had told them 'well done!' when they had obviously tried hard. Instead, I just always wanted more and more from them,' he confessed. 'Ah well, it's too late now,' he continued as he fell into a reverie, doubtless of pupils long gone.

I didn't break into his silence because I found that he had voiced a long buried regret of my own. I too feel that I never praised my sons enough when they were young. I see young-sters today being praised at every hand's turn and that makes me feel quite guilty at times. Then, yesterday, Eoin and I took our customary walk around the farm. He likes me to walk the land with him, exactly as I remember my own parents doing, especially on a fine Sunday after dinner. Often, I am sure my mother would have preferred to put her feet up, with a book, after the job of feeding the lot of us. Still, I never once remember her saying no when Dadda would come in with her wellingtons as a signal of what he wanted. 'You lot be good now,' was all she'd say, as she went with him, to see how the corn was ripen-ing or the bullocks looking.

We went on exactly the same mission, but it was really to see how the second cut of silage was coming along: it was blooming fine, but why wouldn't it be with all the rain we have been having this summer. There is no question of the urea being wasted this year and that's for sure. We use urea here the whole year round despite what the experts say. this is purely because of cost. Unit for unit of nitrogen there are significant savings to be made, and, with one exception, an extremely hot and dry period after the first cut silage, we never saw any advantage in using the dearer product. But we always do listen to experts, Eoin again trotting out his 'must listen to thunder' advice. And so we once tried a paddock with half CAN and the rest with its equivalent in urea. All were unanimous that the urea half grew much better. So that finished that experiment as far as the Kavanaghs were concerned.

Anyway, Eoin and I continued our walk around the land and found some of the beef animals gone astray: three of then had broken into the next paddock where they were not to go for another two days. Of course the rest of them were objecting strongly. saying 'me too, me too', and all congregating by the wire, milling about, churning up the ground. The three breachy ones were just filling their bellies with a self satisfied cut to them, calculated to drive the rest wild. There wasn't a lot Eoin and I could do, on our own, about getting them back again, so we continued on with Eoin saying that he wished that just once he could go for a walk about the land and not find anything wrong.

On our way back home, to get help, we checked the in-calf heifers and lo and behold the first thing we saw in with them was a calf. We do always follow the experts' advice on a leader-follower system when it comes to the young stock. 'God almighty,' said Eoin. 'What if the bull serves her? She's much too small.' The bull wasn't taking a blind bit of notice of the calf, I must say, because the first thing I always check when I go into a field is where the bulls are. I was once seriously chased by a bull and that is an experience I never want to repeat.

So we went as fast as we could to where we knew the lads and Lisa were dosing cattle. We were just in time to chase with them around the field after one bullock that had just jumped out of the cattle race and was pure mad. Isn't there always one like that in every group? Then Eoin told his tales of woe to his son. The thunder suddenly rolled again for me as, very bitterly, Eoin Óg, with a conspiratorial glance at Lisa, said, 'I wish to God that just once the pair of you would come and talk to us about all the things that are going right on this place, and not always be going on about the one or two things you find wrong.... And that bull can't do anything anyway ... that's a bull calf that's broken in to his field... This year I stopped that running the heifer calves in front of the in-calf heifers. Much too often we've had to put up with your so-called accidents....'

'With your way of doing things' wasn't said but it was left hanging there in the air as I could see Eoin Óg was dying to continue in this vein. I'm not sure that the nudge I saw Lisa give him was one of encouragement or to shut him up. Possibly I was being much too sensitive because, still echoing in my ears was the thunder of that teacher's bitter regret, the day before, that he had failed in his job by sparing the praise to his pupils when it was due. We had seen a lot that was right on our walk but not once did we mention that. We had only commented on what was wrong. After Eoin Óg's tirade, Eoin huffily told him and Lisa that he had only mentioned what was wrong for fear they themselves didn't know.

That was true enough, God knows. Still, I do wonder if it was sufficient excuse. And, unfortunately, real damage may have been done with Eoin now swearing that he longer will check things out any more, ever again. They can go to hell for all he cares.... But sure I know he'll forget all about today much quicker than I, and, I fear, Eoin Óg and Lisa.

Visiting Grandchildren (1998)

The reading of the herd test last Saturday was clear — surprise — surprise! In actual fact, however, the all-clear was a great weight off everybody. Eoin Óg rang us on his mobile to tell us once the last cow had gone through the race and hadn't been pulled aside. Of course we have to survive another test in six weeks time. So we had better not get too jubilant, or confident, until then. So I'll say nothing more on that subject for the moment....

There are other subjects I have been warned off, for the moment, as well. If I was to give a little hint, however, it would be to say that it is the best of all possible news, and something that cannot be concealed for ever. I am dying to tell you but I dare not — if I want to live to a good ripe old age.

I could write about my present grandchildren I suppose, even though I also was warned off one happening on that front, also this week. Another lot of grandchildren are coming here today, my three from Dublin, to stay here, with their mother, for a while. Those grandchildren I haven't really seen since last summer. The baby is now walking, I'm told, and like all boys into everything. The girls sound so grown up on the phone that I'll have to get to know them all over again.

So, the next while is going to be busy. Sara seemed a little put out when I told her that they were all coming. It transpired that she was just about to ask me if I'd take the girls for a few days, that she and Pádraig were hoping to get away to visit friends. I, with my big mouth, said that of course we'd fit them in too. But thank God she said no.

Eoin, I know, was more than a little apprehensive already about catering for all the extra mouths and asking how long they'll be staying? He'd really fly off the handle if I said we were having two more little girls as well. As it is he refuses to take more than one of the granddaughters anywhere in the car with him, unless I am also along. One alone, of course, is no bother. But he just cannot cope with children fighting or even bickering.

Last Summer when we had the two American grandchildren staying, even though they were thirteen and eleven, he nearly went into orbit at the constant sniping that went on at times. But then, when they turned into the best of friends, as siblings regularly do, to indulge in some noisy childish game with their young cousins, the noise often drove Eoin out of the house.

Remembering all this, I went and took the initiative, on the phone, and told my daughter-in-law that it is really too much for Eoin. It isn't fair, I said, to expect a seventy two year old to cope with all that extra cooking and cleaning up. You know I hated saying it, straight out, like that. I was afraid of giving offence, you know how it is? I would never have said it in a thousand years if I was on my feet myself. I'd cope, somehow, even if it killed me. Still, there does come a stage in all grand-parents' lives when giving visiting family the full guest treat-ment, with all meals prepared for them, and cleared away after them, plus keeping them entertained all day and every day, proves too exhausting by far.

Now this daughter-in-law appeared to take it marvellously well. I detected no change in the tone of voice at the other end of the phone, as I so often do, when I have said something that offends any of my lot. I wonder do my family read my own tone of voice as well as I read theirs? Helen, with no hesitation, told me that she wouldn't expect anybody to look after her children — she'd bring everything they needed, and also that they'd be fed when they arrived. They were coming to see us, and not to be fed or entertained, she emphasised. In fact, she said, the children were wild with excitement at the thought of coming to see their Granny and Granddad.

I am nervous, however, of how they are going to react to this greatly changed granny they'll find. Last year, when Rebecca was here, Michaella and Nicole came to stay as well and I took them somewhere every single day. We had great fun at the sea, chasing each other with buckets of water. Things are going to be very different this year.

Basically I suppose I made my grandchildren very fond of me, with treats and outings. There was no trace of any of them wanting to go home. Indeed, their parents were more than a little annoyed with me when quite the opposite occurred. The warmth of little bodies clinging to me, not wanting to be parted from me, is necessary to me at some very deep level. Only grandchildren seem to have no objection to coming really close to old bodies. In fact I think that they find some sort of comfort in cuddling up to grandmothers especially. I wonder do we give off some sort of secret aroma that attracts them to us. Stranger things do happen.

And on that note I'll leave you to think about that, and also ask when you last really hugged an older person, especially one disabled in some way? We do still need it you know.

AUGUST

Free For All (1977)

Last week, while washing the delft after the dinner, I spotted a whole lot of strange cattle in our field of winter rape. This was bad news especially because, even at that distance, I knew quite well by the colour of them that they weren't ours. We have no whiteheads, black or red. Everybody else was away for a load of straw, which we had bought at the far side of the parish. So it was totally up to me to get those hungry invaders off quickly before they ate too much of our scarce winter feed. The drought this summer has left the silage pits dangerously low. Hence the field of rape and the travelling so far for good barley straw.

I frantically raced over the farm road, immediately, as fast as I could, to then run and shout and generally wear myself out, trying to hunt those wretched interlopers back from whence they came. Yet, in spite of my roars they kept doubling back to snatch yet another mouthful of the tender, luscious young growth. It absolutely infuriated me to see the young, barely developing plants disappearing down their gullets, roots and all. Finally, with an unmerciful stitch in my side and the blood pounding in my head I was despairing and bitterly resentful of the fact that Eoin had taken the car when they could all have fitted all right on the bale trailer. With the car at my disposal I could at least have gone after them for help, or, better again, gone to the owner of the trespassing cattle.

Resigned to hours of damage limitation, I was never so relieved to see Betty, our neighbour, appearing over our boundary fence. She said that she had just missed their cattle. I strongly suspect, however, that she had heard my screeches — the wind was blowing in their direction. Anyway, in somewhat strained co-operation, and with the very necessary help of her collie dog, we finally got every last bullock back through the hole they had made in our boundary. I, somewhat sharply, remarked how the electric fence wire, on our side, was now all tangled and tossed and no good for keeping anything either in or out.

'God help your head girl,' was all she said. 'Sure our lot don't know what an electric fence is. Four strands of barbed wire is the only thing that lot understand. We never had such a breechy lot of animals. And I wouldn't mind but we only put them in that fresh field today....'

It was on the tip of my tongue to remind her that good fences make good neighbours and it was their responsibility to keep their animals in and not ours to keep them out. That one limp strand of barbed wire her husband had strung from bush to bush after their last trespass obviously wasn't going to work now that their cattle had a taste of what was on the other side. Yet, knowing how easily lasting rows can start over trespass, I said nothing, However, my sour face must have spoken volumes because Betty next said that she'd move them immediately out of that field, and that she'd personally make sure that her husband fixed their side of the fence properly this time — or she'd have his life.

I doubted the efficacy of her threat, however, her husband being one of those know-all yet ineffectual types of men, who, if I was married to him, would be hanging from the nearest limb in no time flat. Eoin would now have to go fencing that night. Eoin, bless him, refuses to fight with any neighbour. All his life he says that he has seen rows that started over nothing much escalate so much out of control that they finish up in the law courts. Inevitably, win or lose, those neighbours are never again on speaking terms. People in this parish have gone to law over the most extraordinary things. And, when Eoin worked for a period in Kerry, he said it was exactly the same there. He recalls one notable case being taken over the continued trespass of a solitary hen.

Anyway, I made my way back home, wearily, through the fields, to the dinner plates still in the sink. Then I saw them, in the short grass, sheets upon sheets of mushrooms, perfect little white buttons, literally in their thousands. Tiredness immediately forgotten I quickly heaped my cardigan high with the bounty. That made little or no impression on the sea of white, however. 'Fás aon oíche', grown in one night, was the old Irish expression for field mushrooms, the only kind of mushroom indeed that we knew in our childhood. I know it isn't strictly true that mushrooms grow overnight. But I swear there were none in that paddock two nights earlier, when the cows were grazing there. And none of the family brought any into me so they hadn't seen them elsewhere either.

The family were in for a real treat that night when I cooked a great big pot-full of the choicest button mushrooms, in milk, thickened with a little cornflour. After supper, all thoughts of fencing were forgotten as Eoin and the lads stretched off, like poisoned pups, so bloated were they with plateful after plateful of this unexpected delicacy. I, myself, was busy with the satisfying task of getting all the remainder into the freezer for later use. They are not as good frozen as fresh of course. Still, by freezing only the very best, they will be welcome during the cold winter months to come as tasty additions to stews and casseroles.

All week I continued to reap my mushroom crop, even getting up at five on Friday morning to get a whole lot of them ready for the Country Market. This paid me well since the customers there practically fought over them. They were quickly swept from the tables and I got orders for over twenty pounds of them for next Friday from people who are afraid they won't get to them before they are all snapped up. So my mushrooms are really a cash crop for me this year.

They didn't just happen, however. In my old home we always seemed to find a lot of mushrooms at this time of the year. Indeed, even when well into our teens, still believing that mushrooms grew only during the hours of darkness, we used to vie with one another to be first up in the mornings. I still remember the chagrin of waking up in the morning to the delicious smell of mushrooms roasting on the old black range, knowing that someone else had beaten me to the draw. I also knew I'd have to be content with the aroma since, as a family, we weren't greatly into sharing. If I was the first up I'd only share with my beloved father. He really loved the full cap mushrooms, sprinkled with salt and cooked straight on the hot stove, gradually darkening and glistening in their own juices.

Ah well! When I married I found Eoin shared the same passion for field mushrooms. But they never grew on the land here. Then, in that first year of marriage, when nothing was too much trouble if it pleased him, during the mushroom season, I made several covert trips to my old haunts, to get a decent feed of mushrooms for my man. As usual, after preparing them I had quite a lot of maggoty ones left over. You know how, when you slice the stem, if there are dark tracks there in the whiteness there is no point in going to the trouble of peeling the cap because there is then bound to be a maggot hard at work up there. So, just as an experiment, I took this waste out to the nearby fields and just threw it about. At the time Eoin laughed heartily at my optimism.

Still, the very next autumn there was a scattering of mushrooms showing in those fields. So then I really went to town on it, gathering overblown as well as good mushrooms on my old home fields just to strew them around the fields around my new home. And we have been getting bigger and better crops of mushrooms. This years beats all, however. I gather this is because of the long drought being followed by rain at the right time. The mushrooms, which are always underground in the form of threads of mycelium, fearing extinction from the drought, are driven to reproduce themselves with the coming of rain and so rush overground to spread their spores far and near. Thus wet summers are poor producers of mushrooms at the back-end.

They also seem to decide for themselves which fields they are going to be in on what years. I cannot for the life of me explain the logic of this. But I do know why there is no use in going too far into any of our fields for mushrooms since they are all in the first half of the field. This is because my bucket of spoiled mushrooms never lasted far into a field. And, being me, I never did get back to finish the job.

However, today I found that the word is out that Kavanaghs have mushrooms in their fields. Now whether this is because I am under constant surveillance or because of my enviable sale of field mushrooms at the market, I am not sure. I strongly suspect the latter, however, because the large group of men, women and children I disturbed today, in my best mushroom field, were utter and total strangers to me. And, would you believe it, they glowered resentfully at me when I proceeded to fill a container for myself and they with bulging bags of my mushrooms. In fact, although not a word was spoken, I was so intimidated by their attitude that I left, discomfited. And you know that never once, in all the years, has either neighbour or stranger been abashed at being caught on another person's land. The attitude, like with us as children, is that whoever is first into a mushroom field had priority rights to the crop. Talk about reaping what they didn't sow.

Of course, before I get into trouble locally, I must say that I have no objection at all to neighbours having a few mushrooms off our land. Why I am now so infuriated with that crowd today is not only because they took my mushrooms but because of what they left in exchange. They dumped rubbish at the gap into the field, where they had parked their cars. I went through the bags hoping to find some identification. I swore to myself that if I did I would take it and dump it in front of their house, picking any flowers they might have there in exchange for my mushrooms. But no such luck. There wasn't a single used envelope in the lot.

We only found their rubbish so quickly because Eoin and I both went out that evening gathering mushrooms for the country market tomorrow. Eoin thought it safer to come with me lest I meet the same sort of pickers again. Anyway, like me, no way was he going to leave all that money growing in the fields for the want of picking. But then Eoin asked me if there was any fear that the mushrooms wouldn't sell in the morning if my pickers from earlier in the day were there at the behest of another market member. That really would be adding insult to injury — and more mushrooms to my freezer than I really want. The boys are at the stage now when they say that they never want to see a mushroom again. And I am rapidly also coming to the same opinion. The freezer, I suspect, will also belch if I try to stuff another bag of mushrooms into it.

The Destroyers (1979)

We are only hopping mad here at the moment. Earlier this year I was giving out about farmers who, when sowing their grain, just cut the plastic fertiliser bags down the sides and then let the wind carry them, where it will, to remain for ever where they finally finish up. Plastic does not deteriorate with time and the wind is no respecter of the neighbours' boundary fences.

Even those plastic fertiliser bags, however, are harmless in comparison in comparison to what we've just found on the land we have rented a couple of miles away. We rented this land in preparation for the upcoming brucellosis blitz on this province next year. We know only too well that we have brucellosis in our cows even though abortions are no longer a storm, but somewhat a more occasional occurrence, on account of the immunity built up over the years.

But, once the Department officials move in and every animal proving positive under test is taken from us, we aim to have these replacement heifers, from clean ground, with no immunity whatsoever, all ready to come into our herd and so keep up our numbers. As it stands at the moment, we will not be allowed buy in any female animals once the official clearance starts. So, we are trying to be one step ahead of officialdom with our young breeding stock already in place. It is expensive, and maybe even unnecessary, because many people tell us that those stringent rules will just have to be abandoned once the Department of Agriculture moves south to the real dairy areas of the country.

Be that as it may, enemies closer to hand may first have destroyed all our longer term plans. Today, Eoin found a dead premature calf in one of those rented fields. And it hadn't just wandered in and died there because it was all stuffed into a jute grain sack, tied with twine at the neck. Eoin only found it accidentally, just inside the roadside fence, when he went to see why some of his in-calf heifers were all congregating at this one point. Somebody had just stopped on the road, evidently, and simply chucked their bag-full of trouble into our field of heifers. Even if it was securely tied into a plastic bag it would have been less of a disease spreader than that jute bag from which all sorts of juices were leaking. Incredible, isn't it, that any farmer in this day and age could do such a thing? Is it any wonder that we are always being warned about the dangers of letting stock drink from any stream or river.

I always thought it unlikely, however, that any man would just throw away dead calves, aborted foetuses, cleanings, or any other kind of dramhaíl into a river, there to float on and infect their innocent neighbours downstream. I must have been extremely naïve, as today's find proved. When somebody could deliberately dump a premature calf into our field there can be no doubt that others can dump their troubles, anonymously, into a river, there to become somebody else's trouble. I suppose they can then plead innocence as they let the river decide where the carcass finishes up.

Our carcass was deliberately dumped on us, however, and I can tell you that if we but knew who it was, acting the informer or not, we'd go all the way with our information. There is enough trouble with foxes dragging carcasses around. To mis-quote a certain politician, however, men who dump dead cattle must be the worst 'mongrel foxes' of all. Still, with all the new rules and regulations inundating us regularly about disease eradication, never have we seen any mention made of these malefactors. Surely they do every bit as much damage as ear-tag switchers. Yet there appears to be no set punishment for the carcass dumpers. How about bringing back hanging?

Putting today's dead calf aside, however, which we seriously hope was an isolated incident and that it was found and the area cordoned off and disinfected before serious damage was done, we are a dirty nation. Just take one look all around you at the unofficial dumps throughout the countryside. Not too far at all from here there is a lovely, little, old, disused quarry — quite a picturesque spot with trees and ferns growing out of precari-ous root holds on the rock face, nature's bonsai. Wild straw-berries thrive on the sunny grassy spots and always I found the earliest primroses here, even as a child. My sons, in turn, thought it a wonderful spot for games of Tarzan or cowboys.

Then, a year or so ago, a miserable so-and-so emptied his dustbins there. Soon, more and more household rubbish was dumped, possibly in the dead of night. Next a scrapped car appeared and then more and more household rubbish was dumped there, quite openly, until the malodorous heap overflowed onto the road. The wind and passing cars are now blowing the loose refuse, starting yet another unofficial dump across the road. The other day I noticed a complete bed-base and mattress there, half out on the road, totally blocking the watercourse. Soon I will be driving through two mountains of rubbish, and, come the autumn rains, over a road destroyed by flood waters. No country child will be picking early primroses there next springtime or, in summer, threading wild strawberries on a stalk of grass, to bring home as a little surprise gift for a parent.

We can't blame all our little troubles on townsfolk coming out to dump their rubbish in out lovely clean countryside, however. Have any of you taken a real good look at the roadsides around your own place recently, by any chance? At Mass, a few Sundays ago, our curate commented that he had counted twenty-one plastic bags on a specified short piece of his road to the church, and forty-three on another. Now, one of those stretches of road passes by part of our farm, so I quickly cocked an ear. And I also got Eoin to drive that way home, certain the reverend gentleman was exaggerating a little for the sake of the effect off the altar. So I also counted the bags. But he wasn't exaggerating. In fact he missed two because I counted twenty-three on that stretch.

There are only nineteen there now, because later that Sunday, I scoured all our own roadside ditches and found four fertiliser bags on that particular piece of road fence. I'd be ashamed to tell you of all the stuff I found on the rest of our road boundaries. And, unfortunately, I had nobody to blame but myself for the peat moss bags in my rubbish collection. I felt very self-righteous, however, about the rubbish I picked up that did not originate from within our boundaries. Now, if everybody in the country did the same for their boundaries, and we really had a clean countryside, perhaps we all might start to respect it. But firstly, we farmers must respect each other's person and property, and refrain from actions which destroy things in any way for our fellow farmers. Begrudgery is really nasty, whatever form it takes. But I never thought I'd live to see the way it took shape for us this week with a diseased calf dumped on our land.

The First Miracle at Ballinspittle (1985)

This week we finally went to see the statue move. The boys, of course, went to the grotto long ago. But I treated the moving statue phenomenon with great disbelief no matter how much I was told. Eoin, as usual, said that I never believed anything anyway so what was new?

'Well! What did any of you see last night?' became the main subject of conversation each dinner time as those who saw something at the grotto went back to disprove the evidence of their eyes. The others, who had seen nothing, just went along for the craic. The daily yarns we've heard out of that place are something else. Each day we have a fresh crop of jokes as we read, in the paper, of moving statues further afield. The lads soon started their own version of the litany starting with:

Our Lady of Ballinspittle — sway for us.
Our Lady of Mount Mellary — sway for us...

I suppose we should have got cross with them, but unfortunately they are really very funny with their mockery into which all visiting friends get sucked. Then the night after Pádraig's twenty-first, last week, the house was still full with those staying on. Fair dues to them they had been very handy that day doing all the cleaning up, the washing of glasses and such. I mention the glasses especially because I was horrified how many short of the count I was of pint glasses when all were boxed up and made ready to go back to the off-licence. I know that it was inevitable that some glasses would be broken, there were so many people here. But I felt that the number missing was excessive and they must be around the house, or garden, somewhere, if they would only look properly for them. But there was nothing for it, I knew, but for me to pay up and look pleasant when the glasses were returned on the Monday. I wasn't averse, however, to letting them all, both family and friends, realise what a poor view I took of this unnecessary extra expense. Parents bear all the expenses of a twenty-first party anyway while the twenty-one-year-old gets to keep all the presents, which seem to get progressively better and better with each son's celebration.

Anyway, the whole gang, boys and girls, gathered here again on Sunday evening, to help us with the leftovers, they said, and then they took the notion to go, en masse, to Ballinspittle. Eoin and I went, thankfully, to our bed. We woke up however, to the sound of great glee in the kitchen and next thing our bedroom door opened to chants of:

'It's a miracle! It's a miracle! They're resurrected...!'

Bleary-eyed we looked at the young faces crowding in all around us, each brandishing several pint glasses. And then I learned that they had only woken us up to tell me that I could now sleep easy, the exact right number of glasses were there for returning, once they had been washed. Through the laughter we gathered that the young people had found them all, scattered all around the hill facing the grotto, in Ballinspittle.

'We just had to clean up the place for her,' said one of the friends and he practically in convulsions laughing. 'I mean it gives the statue a very bad name, that she goes so regularly to the pub for drink, but she doesn't ever take the glasses back with her on her next trip!'

Easily amused they are still, even though all the boys and most of the girls in the gang have now left their teens behind. But even Eoin had to laugh at their graphic descriptions of pints being handed out the back window of the local pub to sustain some of the pilgrims on their walk to the grotto. Although it was well after eleven when they left here to go to Ballinspittle they still had to park simply miles away from the actual grotto itself, so they also had joined in the queue for liquid refreshments out that bedroom window. This probably explained some of their giddiness as they paid me back for my earlier nagging.

Breaking into uncontrollable giggles from time to time, they then went on to tell us stories of the people they had recognised in the absolutely packed grotto. Some were highly amused at some recognised there, with rosaries flying. I noticed, however, in the midst of all the merriment, that when Eoin asked if any of them saw anything a few of them went strangely quiet, including one of our own. And that son did not join in the general laughter either when another lad answered, with a perfectly straight face,

'Well, I don't know about the rest of you, but I was right close up to the grotto when I saw the face definitely change to the bearded face of Jesus. I looked away to see if any of you were around, and when I looked back again, the beard was gone. Then I smelt the very strong whiff of the Veet my granny uses for the hairs on her face ... and then I knew how she had done it so quickly....'

God forgive them, for laughing, and me, I suppose, for using the 'resurrected' pint glasses to fill up my boxes of glasses returned next day to the local off-licence. Still, remembering that son's face, there is a very strong notion at the back of my mind that maybe Eoin and I really should go to see for ourselves.... That son has already been back, twice, that we know of ... and he has been very quiet recently....

The More Rain the More Rest... (1989)

Do you remember last springtime when we were all totally fed up with ourselves, and God, because it just would not stop raining for even one full day and night? I think it was a full three months before we got any kind of a consecutive dry spell and the cows were expensively late getting out to grass. Well, the whole country is now officially in a drought situation, and we are even worse off here than most. What wouldn't we give now, after eleven weeks continual sunshine, for just one day's good rain?

Eoin said, while we were despairing of the rain last spring that we'd pay for it in the summertime. 'This shagging country never knows when to stop raining and when it does stop then it never knows when to start again...' were, I think, his exact words as, through the kitchen window, he watched the rain fall.

While I wouldn't exactly blame it on something in this particular country Eoin does have a point. We always finish up with approximately the same rainfall every year. So, it follows, if we have an excessively long wet period at one time of the year we are bound to have a compensatory long dry period before the year is out. Both extremes bring their own particular problems in farming.

Do you know what, but I'm just sick and tired of problems in farming. Each time I hear the sound of the milk lorry finishing up the milk collection I know quite well that soon they will be into me with long faces and dire reports of how much the milk was down again since the last collection. Eoin is bound to say that if it doesn't rain soon that soon they needn't bother even turning in the cows since it won't be worth anybody's time to milk them. A lot of them have been dried off already in truth. But what can I do about any of this unless I am to turn the water hose into the tank while the lorryman's back is turned? Then they'd soon be in more trouble than ever with our name up for adding water to the milk.

I did draw a bitter smile from Eoin all right when I reminded him of when a prominent farmer was actually caught for such adulteration and all sorts of yarns then went the rounds. My favourite one was that a new farm apprentice was told, on arrival, that the secret of the magnificent cow yields in the herd were the two turnips given to each cow last thing at night. Anyway, when the apprentice was allotted this task one night, the master farmer, on going into the milking parlour, next morning, found two turnips hanging on the water tap in the dairy. Calling the apprentice to account for these he was told that of course he had put two turnips there 'because isn't that the very best cow you have in the place?' An apocryphal tale no doubt that was. I often wonder, however, just who does think up these yarns in the first place. Perhaps some sadist takes pleasure in another farmer's downfall no doubt.

I was accused of sadistic tendencies myself when, one day, I tried to console my menfolk by saying that at least they won't have the usual trouble with quota this year. I was told that was the world's worst thing to have said when I knew how desperate it will be not to be able to fill that last leased quota for which they thought they had paid over the odds at the time. They wouldn't listen to me when I then reminded them that the milk quota year doesn't end until the first of next April, so they will have plenty of time to get extra yields in the cows next lactation. The cows will probably benefit greatly by the longer rest period anyway and may milk much better than usual on calving down again.

But did you ever notice how men are inclined to over react to everything. I know things are bad in that the grass is non-existent, all burned up and dry so that the cows have nothing like enough to eat. But then aren't we getting substantially more per gallon for our milk than we were this time last year. The little or no financial difference in the year so far is surely what counts, what we actually have and not what we could have had if all conditions had been right. The sons still have to learn the lesson that things are never so good that they couldn't be better. Farming is the one game where things are never perfect. If it isn't the weather lets you down it's the price, or disease, or accidental death by misadventure. And always is never enough money to invest in the business. No farmer is ever able to sit back at night and think that he has done a perfect job. He certainly may know that he has done his best, or even better than most. But perfection is unobtainable, by fair means at any rate.

What most aggravates my lot, however, is the hearing of plenty of rain falling elsewhere and others not being as badly affected as we are by drought by reason of type of soil or even geographical position. Rain seems to have fallen just about everywhere else but here if the weather forecasters are to be believed. Their 'threat' of rain just always seems to fizzle out before it gets to us. In those thunderstorms last week the weather station near us actually got almost an inch of rain, while we got nothing but the distant rumbles. So the report on the Journal as to our weekly grass growth was so inaccurate as to be absolutely infuriating. Misery loves company after all.

And I am kind of fed up as well. I am fed up of picking, preparing and processing fruit. It has been a magnificent fruit year with no rain to bring moulds and spoil the crop. So the ripening of the crops has been continuous and non-ending since late June. Even now I still should be out there at the last of the raspberries. They are so ripe and in such perfect condition that they are absolutely begging to be picked. When I was over there for vegetables and potatoes for the dinner I deliberately avoided looking at them so as not to be physically reminded of them.

Old Tom, who worked for us long ago when I was young, if we had more than two or three consecutive fine days, always started to tune, continually:

The more rain the more rest.
Too much fine weather was never the best.

This annoyed the hell out of my father, I well remember, especially when we, his children, joined in. We'd keep it up, however, when the rain was teeming down because then, in the rain, we didn't have to be out all day and every day at this time of the year with blistered and sore hands from stooking sheaves full of thistles.

Too much fine weather is indeed never the best, for man or beast, even today. But I'd better say that quietly, lest those with grain, or on holiday, hear me. Farmers, of course, they say are never satisfied. But the Bible put it best with its prayer to the Lord for the right 'weather in due season'. And we are badly overdue rain right now.... Then I could leave the rest of the fruit rot with a perfectly clear conscience even if it is now too late for the cows to regain their lost milk yield.

SEPTEMBER

Who Stayed my Hand? (1993)

'Do you want to hear a bit of good news for a change?' said Pádraig to Eoin, one morning this week when he met his father mooching about the yard. I was watching Eoin myself from the kitchen window and thinking that his last accident had affected him a lot. There was no spring in his step, no gladness in his demeanour. I idly watched Pádraig walk up to him and then, saw Eoin, inexplicably, throw his arms around Pádraig and the two of them went dancing, in what appeared to be a crazy frenzy, round and around the yard. Then they had a long confab and finally, Eoin, with a decidedly jaunty air, came towards the back door. I, of course, was out it fast to discover what on earth all that in the yard was about.

And it was the best of all possible news. Eoin told me that we are going to be grandparents again.

'And it might be a son this time though I wouldn't say no to another little Missy Michaella either,' he concluded.

'When?' was the first thing I asked of course, naturally enough, and then Eoin warned me that I was to say nothing to anybody because it was very early news yet.

'I don't think that Pádraig was supposed to tell us at all really, but he just could not hold it in. He was bursting to tell someone that Sara was pregnant. So you will be careful, Liz.... They only found out themselves when they used a pregnancy test this morning — so do wait for Sara to tell you herself.'

Eoin, of course, is of the generation when matters of pregnancies were to be talked of in whispers, and discreetly, until

the evidence of it became abundantly clear to all those with eyes
to see. When I saw Sara, however, I didn't need a pregnancy
test to tell me that she was pregnant. She was in the throes of
throwing up. Isn't morning sickness the most dreadful thing?
And the worst of it is that there has been absolutely no improvement in its management over the years. My daughter-in-law is
being given the exact same advice as I got all those years ago
and with the same obvious lack of success too. What is the use,
for instance, of a dry biscuit before you get up in the morning if
the sickness goes on all day and every day. She tried that the
last time, and barley sugar sweets, sour cooking apples, frequent and small meals, etc. and etc. and nothing helped.

We are all very aware of poor Sara being so miserable. Eoin
last night, for instance, suddenly sat up and said he wondered
would that do it. The heroine of his book, borrowed from Lisa,
one of those impossibly beautiful and successful women, had to
be in New York for a business meeting and she was pregnant
and suffering badly from morning sickness. Anyway, she tried
the juice of a lemon in hot water and it worked marvellously.
All sickness disappeared. It is all so easy in books. But Eoin, on
the spot, rang up Sara to give her this advice. I'm sure she was
praying for him because she was sound asleep when his call
came. She says she gets so tired now that she goes to bed the
same time as Michaella. Anyway, she promised Eoin she'd try it
in the morning so we will see if that is any good then.

The lemon will do her no harm anyway. Do you remember
that mad thing there was long ago of us all taking pure lemon
juice, in water, first thing in the morning, as a slimming device. It
was supposed to reduce your appetite for sweet things somehow
or other. I can't say it worked for me any more than did any of
those cures for morning sickness. But once again that makes me
remember an extraordinary happening of my life. I too had been
very, very sick with my first pregnancy. In encouragement I was
then told that morning sickness was never as bad with second or
subsequent children. Fool that I was, I believed this.

Almost immediately I found this to be untrue when dreadful
nausea led me to suspect I must be pregnant again and my first
son only months old. This was 1962, and I was depending on a
combination of breast-feeding and abstinence as a means of

birth-control. Now, the pill was there all right, if you knew the right doctor to prescribe it for medical reasons. It was unthinkable, however, that an ordinary Catholic couple, like us would use it, well not until the Pope had ruled on the subject anyway. The papal encyclical, *Humanae Vitae*, was eagerly awaited by all of child-bearing years. And what a furore it caused in contrast to the non-event of the latest one, which I am afraid I have not read. I cannot even remember its name so that must mean something. I am digressing now I know, but the shift in peoples' thoughts in the time span between the two encyclicals is truly amazing. The last one quite truly has been a non-event as far as my young people here are concerned. They had not even given it a thought when I asked them their opinion on it. Yet I was just at their time of life when *Humanae Vitae* was published and it was of great significance indeed to us all then and caused such a lot of soul searching among us married couples.

To get back to 1962, however, my morning sickness proved to be worse than ever with my second pregnancy. So my local doctor prescribed this new wonder drug for me which was the greatest thing ever. It would stop my sickness and also relax me. My first son was an extremely cross child, crying non-stop, day and night. He had dreadful infantile eczema, so it was hard to blame him even though it was only then that I began to understand, and sympathise with mothers who snap under the strain of an endlessly crying child.

My doctor probably realised how near that dangerous edge I was getting when he said that this new wonder drug, Softenan, would be an excellent sedative for Michael as well. One spoonful for each of us at night and then he said that we'd both get our proper sleep. And Michael could have a spoonful of it during the day too, whenever he was fractious. I got the prescription filled by the chemist and gave Michael a spoon of it immediately. That night, however, when I went to take it myself, the smell of the stuff made me throw up on the spot. I am hopeless anyway about swallowing any liquid medicine. So I did not take any of it. But I continued to dose Michael regularly because it did make him somewhat easier to manage.

Then, one morning, some months later, Eoin's sister came here all fuss and excitement. The night before she had been visiting a friend whose father was a doctor and all the talk there at supper was about this drug, Thalidomide, and its dreadful consequences in babies just being born in several countries where it was distributed under different trade names.

'And I knew that was the stuff you had here!' my sister-in-law concluded dramatically as was her wont.

I listened, but took not a great deal of notice of her, as though my doctor would have prescribed anything in the least harmful to me or mine. I was well on in my pregnancy by this stage, tired and weary, and I continued to give my still fretful child a dose of Softenan every night going to bed. Indeed, I thought no more of what she had said until very much later, and it was very much later, with Seamus, my second son, crawling around the place, when all the publicity about the effects of Thalidomide broke. Then, and only then, I realised quite what a narrow escape we'd had, twice over since I was nearly full term with John by this time and had been just as sick as usual for the duration. And I was still having my prescription for Softenan filled regularly for Michael.

I had no reason really why I had not taken the medicine prescribed for me either pregnancy. I had no knowledge of the potential dangers of taking any medications during the early months of a pregnancy. So it must have been my guardian angel was looking over my shoulder when I had poured out that spoonful of Softenan/Thalidomide for myself that first time. Something too stayed my hand the second time around.

I like to think that it was my unborn child's guardian angel caused me to retch so roundly at the smell, each time. That is a much more comforting thought than the blind chance of morning sickness being all that was instrumental in saving my two fine sons from what could have been a lifetime of deformity. And I still thank God fervently and refuse to consider blind chance.

The Terrible Twos (1996)

Well now things are back to normal here. My granddaughters are home in their own house and once more I can call my time my own. Their parents came back from their holidays fit and well, but missing their darlings so badly.

'Did they miss us?' was the first question asked when we met them at the arrivals hall today.

'Of course they did.' Eoin and I said in unison while stealing a secret glance at each other since we knew in our hearts of hearts that the pair had shown no sign, whatsoever, of missing them. They were too busy running rings around us to do any such thing. Michaella, as always, was a perfect angel. But I could not say the same for the other lassie who is in the throes of the terrible twos. When she was good she was very, very good. But how she can throw a tantrum! I don't think I have ever seen anything like it.

Several times each day she flung herself down on the ground and kicked and screamed until I too was fit to scream at her. I could understand this behaviour if it was because she was not getting her own way. But the tantrums seem to come out of the blue, and always when I wanted to change her nappy or dress her. My face is marked from her objections to that. And the screaming went on and on whether I fussed over her and humoured her, or even if I just walked away and left her for a while. I never had any trouble letting all my sons get over their fits of temper in their own good time. Grandchildren, however, are another matter entirely. I cannot bear to see the little mites so upset.

I do not remember Michaella throwing tantrums. But I do remember one day giving her a quick little tap on her bottom, when, not getting her own way for once, she deliberately kicked me hard on the shin. She was utterly shocked, as indeed I was too, both by the painful kick and my instinctive reaction to it. I quite forgot at that moment that she wasn't mine to chastise. Immediately, however, she was up in my arms kissing me and telling me she was sorry. She is that kind of child, really too soft hearted for her own good. And, most important, she never once did anything like that again.

The other little lady is a quite a different character, however. We had war during the week. And she was at her worst whenever we took her out. She screamed non-stop, and threw herself on the ground, several times, in the supermarket. And I wouldn't mind but I had given her everything she demanded. Honestly, I didn't know which way to turn as so many people were really looking at us. I itched to give her a good hard slap. In public, however, was no place to do that. And anyway, through bitter experience, I already knew that a slap would only make her scream all the harder. She is a very different child to Missy Michaella.

I don't remember my lot either ever throwing tantrums like that. Doubtless they did since all small children go through the 'terrible twos'. With my sons, however, the retribution would have been sharp and hard had they tried tantrums in public. In fact I don't think I could have reared my lot, and survived myself, without the threat of violence, if not the actual practice of it. I never used a stick on them. But I did, on occasion, have recourse to my Scholl wooden sandals. When the sons were creating in any unbearable way I would take off the sandal, bang it on something hard and say that I was counting to three and if they didn't stop, or go to bed, or whatever, by the time I had reached three, I would then use it on them.

They would always be back in line before I got to three. And years later they tell me that they really had no fear of me but the counting to three allowed them to give in easily. Now that there is such commotion about how children were treated in the past I badly needed that assurance. In fact, Seamus, when he was home at Christmas, said that, on the run after them, I was able to somehow kick off the sandal and catch it in my hand as I ran without ever once losing step. He often regales his children with stories of how he was reared so hard. He still thinks it all a great joke, even though he has been known to use a wooden spoon on his own children. He has yet to come to the heart searching phase when you wonder did you really bring them up in the best way possible, or did you harm them in some way, somehow even though you know quite well that you did what you thought was best at the time.

The experts who say you should always reason calmly with children and never ever raise either your voice or your hand, mustn't know quite how impossible children can be. Talking or reasoning with Nicole did no good at all. The same lady says little but understands everything. So I tried a few times explaining, while handing out goodies only to Michaella, that tantrums are about the worst way to go about getting one's own way in anything, that a smile and kiss would get her what she wanted much faster. But do you think she would give in to that method either? Not a bit of it.

It wasn't off the grass she licked that extreme stubbornness, of course. I remember tales told against me of my own childhood. I too, it appears, was wont to throw myself flat on the ground in sheer stubborn temper. But I also had the additional trick of then rolling myself along, not caring where I finished up, dangerous in those days of open fires. I got my come-uppance, however, the day, when visiting my mother's home town of Newmarket, I disgraced her by throwing just such a tantrum and rolling down the main street in my very best clothes. Fortunately, in my progress, I met a chimney sweep. He bent down to me and said he took all bold girls away with him in his black bag.

With the fright of this, and his black face, I wasn't long about running back to my mother's skirts, and behaving myself for the rest of the visit. Now last Friday, in the supermarket, I'd have given a small fortune to anybody, such as that chimney-sweep, who'd frighten my two year old into compliance. But nowadays, of course, everybody minds their own business and ignores bold children. The wider community no longer take a hand when they see the necessity. Anyway, Nicole stopped herself for no reason that I could see, just as it all had started for no good reason either that I could see. So maybe I was all wrong when I said that the girls did not appear to miss their parents in the least while they were gone. Maybe that was the source of her tantrums.

A Snip In Time... (1998)

Sara has just told me that she's had a real clear-out these past few days and all the baby clothes are now gone to St Vincent de Paul. I was holding my youngest granddaughter, Ciara, at the time, having just been given her to admire her first tooth, and I

had commented on how fast she was growing. That was what
had then prompted Sara about the baby clothes and so I was
very glad I had Ciara in my arms, playing with her, so that I
didn't have to make a reply.

My face would certainly have betrayed me if I had to look
up. Of course I am disappointed that no more grandchildren are
intended from that quarter. I would dearly have loved them to
have had a son as well as those granddaughters of ours who are
the dearest things in the world to us. However, they are not the
first couple, for generations past, who gave away the pram and
a year or two later had to go out and buy a new one.

So far, however, three seems to be the thing for my sons: all
those with families have three children apiece. And, whatever
about the rest of them, with one of my away ones, three is all he
is ever going to have. His wife took great pleasure, when they
were here last on holidays, in telling us over a family meal, that
her husband had at last had the snip. Her husband, my son,
said nothing. All the other sons present looked pointedly at me,
to watch my reaction. So I immediately guessed that this was no
news to them. Their wives all kept their gaze firmly directed at
their plates. Eoin was the one, half deaf as he is, who asked
what on earth did she mean by the snip.

'He's had a vasectomy, Eoin. Why should birth control be
always my problem? Anyway, my doctor has advised strongly
against the pill for me...' said the daughter-in-law in question,
her voice holding firm throughout her little speech of justification.

The other lads, of course, then had a field day with unprint-
able remarks about their brother's condition. And, for once, I
was grateful for their banter. It gave both Eoin and myself a
moment to recover our composure. This was the very last thing
we had expected to hear over our dinner table, where we were
all gathered to welcome some of our wanderers home. Just a
few moments earlier I had been commenting on how my family
also all gathered in my old home when any of my siblings were
back to visit my mother.

Actually, I had also been giving a very strong hint indeed, by
saying how great my sister-in-law was, always, then, inviting us
all to a meal together in our old home. My mother really enjoyed
those occasions, with us all around her, and she not having to

lift a finger. She had also had to do it all in her day, however. The feeding of all one's husband's relatives goes with possession of the family home on the farm.

My mother used to get into an awful tizzy when my aunts, the nuns, and my uncle, the priest, were coming for their annual summer visit to their old home. At the time I could never understand why her hand would shake so much when she'd be pouring out the tea from the best silver teapot. But then I got sisters-in-law of my own and fully understood her state of mind.

At least my lot of in-laws weren't nuns with all that entails. My aunts joined an order, La Sancta Union, which never left them set foot in their old home again once they had left it. And, what's more, they left it in the 1920s to go to the order's noviciate in Belgium. It must have been an incredibly hard thing to do, to leave home and family and go to a strange country where they had to converse in a foreign language all of the time. They weren't even allowed to come home to the funeral of either their mother or father.

Then, suddenly, when I was about six or seven, the rules were relaxed and the aunts were allowed to visit their home, but not to set foot inside the house. I remember that there was great commotion moving out the big dining-room table onto the lawn where it was covered with the best white damask cloth. All the wedding-present china was next produced. and there my mother managed to serve a full hot dinner for everybody. The effort wasn't good for her temper, however. I had a sore bottom well before the visitors arrived at all. I can't remember what for, or much about the dinner either. My abiding memory is of my aunts, the nuns, going all around the house, both front and back, peering in every single window to see what changes had been made since they had left. This, I would say, was not foreseen by my mother.

Then, as a grand finale, one aunt insisted that my father, her brother, bring a ladder so that she could once more look in her old bedroom window, pointing out what was now my bedroom window. I can still see her, long black skirts somehow hitched up to her waistband, flying up that ladder. My mother had a bothered face. Without seeing she was only too well aware of the likely cut of my room. Fair dues to that aunt, when back on terra firma, ruffling my hair, she laughingly commented that she was glad to see I was no tidier than she had been in her day. That comment probably saved me from getting another sore bottom when they were all gone away. And I, in my turn, made no comment whatsoever, when at a family gathering at my old home, I saw that my niece, who then occupied that room, was no tidier than the two generations in it before her.

But back at my own family dinner table, for which Eoin and I had done all the preparation, I couldn't help but think how very much times had changed. I also wished that it wasn't far too late for me to administer a good hard slap to more rear-ends than one at my table. But what's done is done....

Share Your Pain (1998)

Yesterday, 17 September, the anniversary of the day I fell and broke my back, found me going to my new doctor. I was going into hospital for the second time to have injections into my spine while under full anaesthetic. But I struck before I arrived there. It had helped so little the last time that I suddenly wondered why I should put myself through it all once more. There had to be another way. I am so tired of putting a good face on things, always being the brave, cheerful soldier, taking everything on the chin. Sometimes, instead, I have felt great resentment at what has happened to me. My sense of loss is very real, my pain sometimes practically unbearable.

Yet, with everybody I have played the game of never-say-die, a perpetual smile plastered on my face. I knew only too well that nobody, except Eoin, wants to hear how I really feel and yet he is the one I must not burden with my self-pity. It had come to the stage when even all my sons never asked me how I was: they'd ask their Dad instead and he'd say, 'fine really'. At times I felt the need to tell them the truth. They, however, did not really want to know of my anguish, physical or mental. A lot of my other visitors were much the same. You know that old joke about the bores people can be when you ask them how they are and they proceed to tell you, when all you were really doing was making polite conversation.

People just don't want to know about anybody's pain except their own. It became something of a joke with me, keeping my X-rays at my bedside, so that if I got really annoyed at being told how great I was and that I'd be perfect again in no time, I could then force my visitors to look at my X-rays and make them see precisely all the metal that is screwed into my backbone, keeping me together. That, I'd hope, might make them understand why, despite their exhortations, I just could not take up my bed and walk. Really though, a year later, I now wonder, apart from my little game with my X-rays, if I did not all too easily pander to the fact that most people did not want to hear of my ongoing pain. It must have been a great comfort to all my visitors to find a cheerful Liz when they called. Then, all they had to do was to say things like if anybody could get back to a normal life once more, I could.

They did not want to acknowledge my real sense of loss, and fear that I would never again be able to live a fully normal life. And, of course, I too basked in the fact that people said how wonderful I was to be such a gutsy fighter, always cheerful and smiling. Any sign of me falling off my self-imposed pedestal and I'd quickly be told of others who had been injured much worse than I. I even had Superman, Christopher Reeves, quoted at me more than once, with comments on his television appearances, his book, and how great he was about being totally and utterly paralysed. So, what I am really wondering is whether all this best foot forward stuff, no pun intended, really, on his part as well as mine, is really a good thing. Perhaps a little vulnerability, the sight of a little pain, may also help others to cope. I, personally, got so sick of the kind of self-help books that quote things like: 'there is no such thing as a weak body, only a weak mind.'

This applies to our nearest and dearest too, the carers. They too have a great loss to grieve, especially after their loved one has lost a limb or had a stroke. Not alone has the victim's life been totally changed but so too has theirs. They also must be allowed a little space to grieve and show their pain. I know from someone who has lost a limb that it does not always help to have people telling them how wonderful modern prostheses are now and how well others have coped. I also have seen both wives and husbands coping with the dire after-effects of a stroke on their partners. They too need a listening ear to their tales of frustration especially if the patient just does not seem to be trying quite as hard as others feel they should. Maybe we should, just now and then, wipe that cheerful grin off our faces and tell how it really is. Our stories do not have to be uplifting at all times, just so that others feel easy with us. There is comfort for other sufferers in knowing others too feel pain, at all its levels.

That doctor told me, when I phoned to say we weren't going to the hospital this time, that there are other ways of managing my pain even if it cannot yet be stopped entirely. He then said that, considering my injury, I had made a most remarkable recovery, and how difficult this must have been at times, especially this first year. It was incredible the relief to my spirit those words, over the phone, were. At last my pain, both physical and mental, was acknowledged officially. So, is it any wonder that I immediately made an appointment to attend his pain clinic next week. I did tell him, however, that if it didn't work reasonably quickly, I would not be back. I shall need more than those few soft words of balm for my mind. I shall also require balm for my poor old body.

An Anonymous Tip-Off (1997)

'Here we go again!' I thought bitterly as I closed the door behind the district veterinary officer, and wondered how best to break the news to Eoin and the lads that our endless rounds of herd tests were about to start all over again. I pondered whether it would be better to go and find them and come straight out with the news that there was another brucellosis breakdown in the area, or should I wait a few hours until they had their dinners in peace? There was no way, however, to soften the blow. All I could buy would be time.

Of course once I saw that particular man at the door I knew

it meant trouble. He was here again last year when our next door neighbour had that dead calf which proved to be brucellosis positive. Then we had the most awful worry until our next test proved negative, as did the our next two tests as well. So, quite honestly, brucellosis was the last thing on my mind. My immediate reaction was that it was that last lot of bullocks which finally went to the factory that were bringing him out, that we were gone down with TB once again. But I was wrong.

How I hate to see any government officials at my door. I don't think one of them ever came with good news for us. It is always a question of us having to account for ourselves in some way or another and recently we seem to have had quite a spate of such officials calling. It started with a pollution officer who had got a complaint about us. The next was our local Department man. You will hardly believe it but this official was out to us because headquarters in Dublin had got a letter saying that we, the Kavanaghs, were importing stock from England and that we were overheard 'blowing' that we didn't give two damns about BSE, the Department, or anybody else either.

Except that it was September I would have said that it was an April Fool's joke someone in head office was playing on your man. But it was no joke. Someone had really gone to the trouble of writing such a daft letter, but didn't sign it of course. And there was, I believe, no further information about precisely how we were bringing in those animals. So the official was out to find out how!

'We brought them into the country in our private yacht, the one that sleeps twelve, an animal to each bunk, I suppose,' quipped Eoin sarcastically.

But whole thing was so preposterous that I really had to laugh. The sons on the other hand were mad out, ready to go for somebody's windpipe, if they but knew whose. But the official wasn't telling. Now, lest you think that we have bad neighbours, that this sort of thing doesn't happen anywhere else, or to anybody else, you had better think again. When Eoin said 'Why us?' we were told that all government offices regularly get anonymous letters, even if not ones quite as bizarre as ours, as if we, or indeed anybody else either, could side-track regulations to the extent of smuggling in cows.

It also appears that at the end of the quota year, and this year was worse than most, the Department of Agriculture, and the co-ops, are literally snowed under with messages about milk being moved at dead of night from A to B or vice-versa. And those who take quota without using the land as well, all have somebody acquainting the authorities of the fact. Some busybody picks up the telephone or puts pen to paper. It seems all wrong that anonymous 'tip-offs' send government personnel tearing through the country. In the bin is the obvious place for such correspondence. But then again, in this particular case, BSE is such a serious matter that you can understand Dublin getting in a flap about it, anonymous letter or not and our good record.

We, of course, told your man that we have never imported any animals in our lives, not to mind right now. We don't even buy in any animals, except bulls, being a totally self-contained herd. And he seemed to accept our word for it. So what purpose was there in his coming out at all beyond acquainting us of the fact this anonymous letter had been received at head office? If we had been up to anything we would hardly have admitted it to him surely. And he could not detect an English cow from an Irish cow just by looking at her, any more than you could tell an English from an Irish person by sight alone. 'Unless, of course, English cows moo with a different accent?' said I, also being sarcastic. Or do Dutch cows sound different again? Eoin and I intend to go to Moorpark next week, to see their experiments on imported animals, so that's a question I can ask!

I'd be far more likely to get a sensible answer to that question than trying to find out who specifically has it in for us, or how can the Department knows about the movement of animals unless one turns up in a herd test with an unexplained ear tag. He did let us know, however, that we had every reason to be running scared about brucellosis again. The neighbour who is now in trouble, is at the other side of us from the neighbour in trouble last year. So, if there was transmission of infection, was it through our land? We were told last year that we would have to have a whole series of tests because infections could take up to twelve months to show up. So now we just have to sweat it out all over again?

Our last brucellosis test was on 15 January this year. So there's another worry, what our vet is going to charge per head. And the price of milk is down. What ever will be next? And maybe those bullocks to the factory aren't out of the woods yet? A TB infection in the herd would just crown things right now. You know the feeling when people say that they are just waiting for the other boot to fall? Well, the longer I live the more I wait for that other boot, the next government official at my door. There is no such thing as peace of mind farming anymore.

Did you ever think about how our lives are now controlled? It isn't so long ago that the fear of sin and the eyes of the neighbours were enough to keep us all in order, and on the straight and narrow. From our earliest days, parents, Church and schools, socialised us into doing right. Fear had a part to play because, as we were learning right from wrong, choosing wrong usually meant a physical punishment. Pretty quickly we were trained to do what was right purely because of our fear of sin and what the neighbours might think. The desirability and benevolence of such social controls were never questioned. The state hardly entered into the analysis at all beyond checking that one had a light on one's bicycle and that the rates were paid. Farmers got on with their lives and nobody paid them a blind bit of notice.

But nowadays, there is such a proliferation of information, surveillance and security systems in place that we can actually talk about the panoptic power of the state, where the few watch over the many. Panoptic is a fancy term for power through surveillance and is taken from a form of prison, the panopticon, designed by a chap called Bentham way back in the last century. In the prison panopticon the prisoners were put into individual cells, lit by windows back and front and artificially all night long. These cells were in a circle all around a central guard tower, so that all the prisoners could be supervised simultaneously. As a consequence the prisoners knew they could be under surveillance for all or any of twenty-four hours a day, but had no means of knowing, for sure, if in fact there was even a guard in that watch tower at all. Hence they came to behave as if under the constant surveillance of a warder. And, totally separated from each other, they had no way of knowing how others were behaving. Such knowledge might encourage their disobedience and/or their taking a calculated risk.

Farmers today are like those prisoners. We are the ones in those cells, lit back and front, always open to surveillance but never quite sure whether we are being personally watched or not. We have that spy in the sky watching us, with its heat sensors for any animals placed on a field for which set aside is claimed, or to check if indeed the fields where grain is growing correspond with the map sent in to the central watch tower. There is also that central computer which keeps track of every animal, from birth to death, so if we sell an animal, that computer, just like a fat spider in a web, gets a tug on an information line to record that fact. It will also inform the guard if an animal from a locked up herd, turns up in somebody else's herd test without all the forms being correctly processed.

Then, for those who employ outside help, there are all kinds of paper trails which track them down. If a farmer gives a contractor, of any sort, more than £3,000 any year, the full details you have to supply alert another fat spider of a central computer. Something similar happens when you apply for VAT refunds. But worst of all, the spider we most dread, rightly or wrongly, is the tax man, who has the best spun, and most central web of all, which traps every bit of information passing by his central lair of a watch-tower.

Now am I exaggerating when I say all of that? And I haven't even mentioned the Department of Agriculture inspectors who are checking all the milk entries in the co-ops to see if there are any sudden, unexplained rises in milk production, caused by any illegal trafficking in milk coming up to the end of each year. And what about those checks in meat factories and the export boats. The list is seemingly endless. That is what keeps us truly in line knowing all those checks are there. Indeed we, as farmers, only become aware that we are being watched through reports in the media. The media are thus responsible for empowering this belief system, that we are under surveillance, which in turn is necessary to support a system of panoptic control.

Take for example that ultimate horror, a revenue audit. If the news hits the newspaper, as in how much somebody had to pay up, the first thing that runs through our minds is whether we have had any dealings with same person and could there possibly be a connection to us. I can think of nothing more horrible than to have been engaged with something not quite above board, taxwise, and then hearing that person has had an audit. Then you would know fear, raw unadulterated fear. That kind of fear, of constant, unremitting, perfect surveillance, is what is being used to keep us all in line these days. Was the fear of hell fire ever that bad?

OCTOBER

Neither a Borrower nor a Lender... (1997)

Tempers were very frayed here this morning and one word out of place from me and all hell would have been let loose. So I refrained from saying, 'neither a borrower nor a lender be', even though I was sorely tempted.

Still, that advice is just as relevant today as it was in Shakespeare's day. One of the few things about Eoin that annoys the hell out of me is the fact that he is too nice, at times, to other people. He is utterly incapable of saying no to anybody who comes here with a hard luck story, wanting to borrow something he has, be it either a bull or a farm implement.

But that was not what caused him to suffer, badly, today. Today's trouble was caused by a nameless neighbour, who, some weeks ago, borrowed our fertiliser spinner for just an hour or two. I was there when he came a-calling and so heard the long preamble to why he needed our fertiliser spinner so very badly. He told of how the agricultural advisor had just been to him and said that if he didn't give his new grass seeds a top dressing of nitrogen, immediately, they wouldn't survive the winter. He only then added that the spout of his own spinner had got damaged — he'd be weeks waiting for spare parts — so could he have ours for just that one job? Quite how that damage occurred to his own machine was glossed over.

Also conveniently forgotten was our harrow which came back with several tines missing and the fact that Eoin had to go to that man's house himself to collect our car trailer only last week. Borrowers have an enviable, happy-go-lucky attitude to life. Not alone are they so sure that they won't be refused, with that trusting puppy look down flat, but they also seem to have no worries about anything going wrong with the borrowed object while in their possession.

Eoin, on the other hand, is a bag of nerves the few times he has borrowed something, lest any damage happen for which he is responsible. He says that with his luck anything near breaking point will break with us. It never fails all right. We've had a burst tyre on a borrowed tractor whose replacement cost us dearly. And the one and only time he borrowed a horse-box his mare burst through the front of it, all because he hadn't put some bar or other in place before loading her. He could nearly have bought a second hand box for himself by the time the borrowed one was fully restored to its original mint condition. The lender in this case came off by far the best of his generosity to Eoin the borrower.

In damage limitation, before he said yes that day, Eoin warned your man to be sure and wash out the spinner, thoroughly, when he was finished his spreading because nitrogen cakes badly and corrodes everything it touches even if only left in the spinner just overnight. 'Of course I will,' came the somewhat testy reply to which I was witness. 'Don't I always, without fail, do that with my own?' He was really huffed at the implied suggestion of neglect. I'd say he was even more offended when Eoin pointedly told him to be sure and bring it back — this time. A sniff was his only reply as he hitched his tractor up to our spinner and drove off out the yard, quickly, belching smoke.

We have now finished putting out our own nitrogen for this year, so, even though all this occurred a full ten days ago, neither of us thought of our spinner again until the 0.7.30 was delivered last evening. Eoin decided to start putting it out first thing in the morning since the ground conditions are still quite good. And putting it out now lessens the risk of grass tetany in the Spring, as he explained to me over breakfast. He then went out to hitch up to the spinner — to find no spinner in the yard. Then, and only then, he remembered he had lent it to that neighbour. Fuming, he drove into the man's yard to collect it himself. I'd say there was smoke coming out of his ears as he knocked on their back door.

'He's not back from the creamery yet,' the wife informed him. 'But I dare say your spinner is up in the haggard some-where along with the rest of the stuff.'

And so it was, among other discarded bits and pieces, some of whose outlines could only be guessed at with the fine growth of overblown nettles. One piece looked familiar, however, as indeed it should. Eoin was mortified to find our field roller there, where it obviously had been for months, and we had never even missed it. Eoin also swears that he never lent it, and, when he came home, asked me if I, by any chance, had done so. I hadn't, of course. Borrowing and lending is 'men's work' and the 'little woman's' permission is never required.

Anyway, Eoin filled up with 0.7.30 and went off to start his day's spreading. But he was back in no time flat because not a granule of the fertiliser would come out the spout when he put the spinner in gear. He had to come home again and start empty-ing the lot out with buckets, not the most pleasant of jobs and very hard on the hands. Then, and only then, he found the base plates were completely and utterly corroded, stuck fast. Tom had obviously used it, never washed it out, and then left it to rot in the haggard. What did it matter after all when it wasn't his?

I passed by the workshop just a while ago, but I did not go in. I knew, from the language polluting the autumn air, that Eoin had cut his hands yet again as he struggled to free the plates. I also know that if the 'prayers' Eoin was saying for Tom land on his head no way will he live to see another dawn. Which, in fact, might be easier for him than to face Eoin when he heads up there tomorrow to collect his 'borrowed' roller.

A Day Out — For All the Good That Did...(1996)

'Come, on Liz, it will be a day out for you!' said Eoin, when I first demurred at the thought of going with him to the Tatter-salls sale. 'Some day out!' I thought, despairingly. But, of course, I never voiced my opinion because I dare say there are a lot of wives who would dearly love their husbands to want them along too at all times. And also, poor Eoin has tagged along

after me, often enough, visiting gardens this year, so I'd feel
very badly about not going along with him when he asked me.

'You can always go off and look at some gardens in Co.
Meath while I'm at the sale,' Eoin then coaxed sensing me
weakening.

'True enough,' I again thought to myself. 'But fat chance I'd
have of going off to look at gardens, even if I knew where to
look. He'll want me there all the time and God knows what that
sale will be like!'

So that is how, and why, I had my day out this week, at
Tattersalls, for all the good that did me, Eoin, or our four-year-
old filly. We are all three home again with nothing whatsoever
achieved. It was a most depressing day, and a mighty boring
day too, sitting there, hour after hour, as horse after horse was
brought into the ring and auctioneers tried to coax bids from the
audience.

Prices were shocking bad. I know only too well what stud
fees cost. And time and again I saw the price offered for animals
much less than the owners must have paid for the services of
the stallion, not to mind all the costs after that. Everybody there
said the bad prices were due to the BSE scare. Nobody was
buying horses. There were none of the usual lot of English
buyers around, it appears, since it is the cattle men who are also
the fondest of their horses. They, after all, are the ones who have
the most time for races, point-to-points, hunting, and the like.

Cows and horses don't mix so well. Maybe that is why I
have no particular liking, or knowledge, of horses. There were
always cows on the farm throughout my childhood. As long as I
can remember the dominant refrain in our social life has been,
'Must be home in time to milk the cows.' It didn't matter where
we were. At the sea, on the beautiful hot Sundays of my childhood, my mother would round us all up, overcoming our
reluctance to leave the water, with the usual refrain of 'time to
go home to the cows'. And we would reluctantly dress, knowing we were going home only to face into work, just as most
people were arriving after their leisurely Sunday lunches. We,
as a family, would have gone off to the sea immediately after
Mass and a quick bite to eat.

Actually, my mother was the one who always brought us.

My father never went to the sea with us. He'd go for a stretch on the bed instead, every Sunday, I suppose tired out after a week of up early to milk the cows. Yet, as a young man he, too, was keenly interested in hunting, according to the stories he told us. My mother was the one who brought the cows with her, there always having been a dairy herd on her home place in North Cork, where there were many of the landed gentry class. In those days, in my father's area, the local fox hunt was mostly farmers, it appeared, not like today. The last day the hunt passed over our land, which they now rarely do because of all our electric fences, Eoin came in, quite cross, saying that there wasn't one face he knew now among the whole bleddy lot of them. And he, before we got into cows, was a very active member of that hunt himself, as was his uncle before him. With the uncle, who never married, the horses were the last thing to go. He bred horses too, so you could say the disease is in the place.

A frightening number of the horses at the sale did not go to new owners, our one included. Our filly was very late indeed on the sale list, and a blind man could see that it was a lost cause long before her turn came. Eoin got more and more determined that he was not going, as he said, 'to give her away', as he discussed options with other horsey men. I eventually stayed, with my book, in those comfortable seats, while Eoin traipsed in and out to her box. I must admit too that at one stage I fell fast asleep, with the heat and the monotony. But I got a rude awakening when Eoin sat down again beside me and said brusquely, 'Come on Liz! The filly is boxed. We're heading for home. There was no point in staying any so and so longer here. We'll get a good piece of the way in daylight if we start now.'

I said nothing, because as I keep saying I know nothing whatsoever about the mysteries of horses. If it was anything to do with cows, our livelihood, it would be quite a different story. I don't interfere with Eoin's hobby, no matter what I may think. Instead I just try to make the right noises at the right times.

So, since I thought it wisest, on the way home silence prevailed, until we were held up at the traffic lights on the Naas dual carriageway. Then, I noticed on the far side a cross and bunches of both withered and fresh flowers. All at once I realised this must be where poor Veronica Guerin was murdered and, with a sense of shock, pointed it out to Eoin. Then, God forgive me, came my first laugh of the day. Waiting at the traffic lights, Eoin blessed himself, in the normal orthodox fashion, as he would passing a church, but out loud, since, like the rest of Ireland, our personal helplessness in the face of terrible evil and wrong, upset us greatly.

But somehow, here, Eoin's 'In the name of the Father and the Son...,' became: 'In the name of the Father, and the Son ... and the murdering hoors and bastards,' as he continued, touching his right and left shoulders fully in his depth of feeling. And all I could do was laugh and laugh as he looked uncomprehendingly at me. Then I blessed myself in precisely the same way as he had done and we were both bent over laughing and all the tensions of the day were released.

Which was fine for us. But did nothing whatsoever for that weight of horseflesh in the trailer behind us.

A Sell-By Date (1995)

Autumn is afire in my garden, the season of mists and mellow fruitfulness, and all that Keats said so much better than I ever could. Isn't it funny how the words learned by rote at national school stay with one for ever, and can sometimes even be a bother when the rest of the quotation won't come. My family look blankly at me if I then ask them for help with the words, because that is not the way they were taught. But sometimes the beauty of autumn catches me by surprise and sadness, and snatches of poetry, even if written well nigh two hundred years ago, reassure me that I am not alone in feeling as I do.

For some reason, this autumn is particularly magical yet nostalgic, basically because the good Lord sent us rain and sun in due season and such an excellent harvest. Now, as never before, again to quote Keats, my mossed old trees are bending with apples and all fruit is filled with ripeness to the core. In his perfect picture of autumn, however, Keats said nothing of the wasps hollowing the skins of the late plums, the early grapes, and just about everything else they can land on, all the things which should have been safely harvested and gathered in by now.

That perhaps is what gives me the real catch in my heart, the vexed question of life's sad satiety and surplus. Once again I am reminded that the real pleasure is in the endeavour, the yearning, in the waiting and not in the having. Figs are ripe on their warm south wall. Even my lemons, my first crop ever, after years of trying, are yellow, echoing and rivalling the huge globes of the pumpkins, which were never bigger and better. Yet nobody likes figs except myself and what can one do with several hundredweights of pumpkins. Then, to crown it all, I saw foreign grown apples, all smooth, red and uniform, in a daughter-in-law's fruit bowl during the week, the shop seemingly nearer than the orchard.

Of course, if I had any sense, waste would not bother me at all, especially when it isn't costing me anything personally. But it is hard to break the habits of a lifetime. Even the bread board, when I was young, had the motto, Waste Not, Want Not engraved on a border around its edge. Nowadays, bread-boards probably have a sell-by date attached.

That expression, a sell-by date has entered the vocabulary of all the young people I know, which is fine when seeking out the freshest item in the supermarket. There, what is out to the front is often yesterday's bread, milk or whatever. But, when I hear of perfectly good clothes being described as past their sell-by date and only fit for the dump, I shudder, and entertain serious thoughts of raiding that dump of ours.

However, a young man, when recently I idly asked him about his love life, took the biscuit as far as I was concerned, when he described his girlfriend to me as being past her sell-by date now as far as he was concerned. At least it wasn't a wife he was talking about. Although that reminds me of a great put down I heard during the week. In company, when we were talking about how long we are all married now, this husband commented that it was high time he traded his wife in for a younger model, a joke men often make. But she, quick as a flash, somewhat scornfully replied, while looking him up and down, 'That's right, love. We can all see for ourselves that you haven't a hope of trading up.' And, since we could all indeed see that he was well past his sell-by date, with a big beer belly on him, the laugh was well and truly on him.

Now, gardens well furnished with trees should never have a sell-by date, despite fashion and generational changes. That, I think, is why Autumn always catches me out in that I did so much there and yet I did not do enough. My one big regret is that I did not plant more good trees when I was younger. In semi-maturity they would have meant much easier gardening now that I am older, as well as being a great source of pride and consolation. I know that is an odd thing to say. But, at those frequent enough times when I wonder what I have really done with my life, a walk around my garden assures me that at least I created some beauty and utility which will outlive me.

To make doubly sure of that I have also threatened the next generation that I will come back to haunt them if they ever dare to bring in a bulldozer to 'my' garden. I put the 'my' in inverted commas, because, when you are dead, nothing, not even your body, belongs to you. That is then the legal property of your next of kin, to do with as they wish. I want to be buried in my garden when I die but I don't fancy my chances there. Now that's a sobering thought for a glorious autumnal day.

But Michaella will remember my garden. 'This is a magic place, Diyee,' she suddenly said to me yesterday, all bright eyed with excitement. We had been chasing butterflies, eating grapes, picking autumn raspberries and examining how her name was growing on her very own pumpkin, as if carved in relief, as a result of us cutting it into the skin some weeks ago. The capacity of a child for wonder is marvellous. Everything is in the here and now. These glorious late Autumn days don't, for her, mean that winter is coming. Instead, now that she is at the stage of counting everything, we counted all the different fruit she has picked, and enjoyed, in my garden during the year, ever since the first early strawberries in the tunnel.

Then, together, we started planting up the first lot of indoor strawberries for next year in their containers, which are discarded plastic drums from the farm, cut lengthways and given drainage holes. And I was suddenly happy again. Nothing here, myself included, has a sell-by date, if I am left have my way.

I Was a Daughter-in-Law Too... (1995)

Last month, during the Ploughing Match, one father and son came to see me, and the father was delighted with life, having just got his first EU retirement cheque. He was walking on air saying that the young lad can have all the worries now.

'Did you lease your land to him, or sign it over?' I asked, out of pure curiosity, since in this case 'the lad' looked just that, a very young man indeed and the father, himself, was far from the normal retirement age.

'I signed it all over, on the dotted line, and it's the best day's work I ever did because himself here, won't see me wrong. There'll always be a corner for me. And sure haven't I got him well trained anyway? He's farming with me full time now since he was fourteen when he decided he'd had enough of school,' came the fast reply from the father as he put his arm publicly around his son.

And, since the son made no attempt to pull away, the relationship between father and son appeared to be really good. So why did I suddenly feel nervous for them, especially when I heard that this particular young man did not even have a girlfriend yet, not to mind a wife. I know I am getting much too cynical in my old age because my immediate reaction was that it will probably work out, but only if there isn't a mother there to be a mother-in-law.

My cynicism has been fuelled, I fear, by all those letters to the *Journal* lately, on mother-in-law/daughter-in-law relationships. To tell you nothing but the truth I found them all downright depressing, with only one or two honourable exceptions. I have been sure, these past years, that I get on reasonably well with my daughters-in-law. But, on reading those letters I began to wonder if I have been kidding myself all these years? In actual fact, maybe they really hate my guts but they are just too polite to ever say so?

But, against that, the highlight of the ploughing match to me personally was when Lisa came into the *Farmers' Journal* stand and, on overhearing something complimentary being said about me in the crowd, she said she'd tell Liz that. The woman in question then asked did she know Liz personally. And Lisa replied that she ought to, since she was Lisa, her daughter-in-law. All sorts of questions then came flying, fast and furious, or so Lisa told me afterwards. This was the highlight of the show to me because, if I am really hard on my daughters-in-law, as some accuse me of being, would Lisa have so willingly volunteered that information back to me, or, indeed, who she was, to them?

To get back to those letters, however, the one thing that really interested me is that no complaining mother-in-law ever makes reference to what kind of a daughter-in-law she herself was in her own day. Have they all faced up to their own guilty consciences, I wonder, before they let their angry words fly? I know, personally, that there are certain things I did when I was a new young wife that still, to this day, make me hot under the collar to remember. But remember them I do. What is even worse is the way I remember that, at the time, I felt fully and utterly justified in my bad behaviour.

So, whenever a daughter-in-law of mine does or says something that annoys or hurts, which does happen from time to time, make no mistake about that, I take out those blush-making memories while still keeping the zip tight shut on my lip. Then, in the comparison, my annoyance or hurt of the moment is put in perspective. My daughters-in-law are no different than I was in my day. So it is easy for me to be understanding, even though I know quite well that a confrontation, and not understanding, is what the young people really crave. I, instead, always force myself to remember what it is like to be young, newly married and finding one's feet in marriage as in life.

It is only since I stood in her shoes myself that I even once considered how my mother-in-law might have felt about things I did and the changes I made when I married her only son. Before, I just thought about how I felt. Such is the conviction of the young that the world revolves about them. I then felt that Eoin was, and should only be, my husband, full stop. I never went as far as articulating this point of view, no matter how I festered inwardly, simply because, like my daughters-in-law, I was much too polite. Still I bet that I was as easy to read as an open book.

I am very glad now, however, that I always kept my mouth shut. A friend of mine recently told me how she still blushes to remember the day her resident mother-in-law was giving out to her son, my friend's husband, about something he had done or not done. My friend then got on her high horse and roundly attacked the poor mother-in-law saying how dare she talk like that to 'my husband'. Billy did not come into the equation at all. He was just the battleground. The battle was for ownership, which cannot be shared after marriage.

I always joke that before each of my five sons got married, their girlfriends courted me as well as my sons and we had joint ownership. But, on walking down the aisle, immediately after the wedding ceremony, each bride had an invisible notice affixed to my son's back, especially for me to read. And that hypothetical notice read, in big bold capitals:

DON'T YOU EVEN LOOK AT HIM — HE'S MINE!

Then, while that notice stayed up, I, as a mother, could not straighten that son's tie, knock a bit of fluff off his suit, or even pass a comment on his choice of tie with that suit, without giving offence, even though never a word might be said. The body language speaks volumes always. And that situation continued until the girls in question decided, of their own volition, to take off that notice. The time periods, in my case, varied from two years to ten years. But down they eventually did all come.

However, my unresolvable problem is that my mother-in-law did not live long enough for me to take down the notice off Eoin's back. That, I deeply regret.

Real Road Rage (1995)

Eoin and I had our first episode, recently, of real road rage. Well, I had better qualify that statement quickly and say that is was our first episode of road rage outside our own car! Poor Eoin, he always meets the world and all of B & Bs whenever we're driving anywhere. And I don't mean places where we could stay for the night. His B & Bs are all the bitches and bastards sharing, or, rather not sharing the road with us.

Nothing is more certain to throw my quiet man into a rage than the white line huggers. There we'd be, cruising along, smooth as could be, when we'd catch up with a car clung as tightly as possible to the white line in the middle of the road. Which is all right on a narrow road, since they are then giving equal way to oncoming traffic. But it is far from all right, on the good main roads, when there is room inside them for at least a lorry, or even two side by side, to pass.

'Another f****r who doesn't use his mirrors,' fumes Eoin if we are more than five seconds stuck watching that white line hugger, who has his eyes firmly glued on the road ahead and quite oblivious, seemingly, of us up his rear end. Normally, drivers instinctively note a car behind and the quick flick of the eyes checking this fact, is obvious in the side mirror to the car behind.

When flashing his lights is to no avail, because of the non-use of mirrors by the driver in front, Eoin has real difficulty being content with tucking himself in behind until a pause in the oncoming traffic allows him to pass out in safety. I used to waste my breath telling him to be patient, that it was the way that the poor devil in front was so nervous, that hugging the white line gave him, or indeed her, confidence. But, I long ago found out, silence works better in cooling the temperature within the car.

We were in kind of a hurry, being a bit late that day, when, on a grand wide piece of the road, we met a fine example of the species, the white line hugger. Eoin went through the usual rigmarole of approaching, waiting, and then light flashing. But this young man was indeed using his mirrors, because he immediately gave us a two fingered salute out the open window, in response, and then deliberately drove over still further onto the white line, even straddling it at times, while increasing his speed.

There was an oncoming steady stream of traffic, so Eoin was happy enough, slipping back slightly, the increased speed meaning we should still get there in time. But then the driver of the car in front of us suddenly jammed on his brakes, giving me the fright of my life as Eoin braked sharply in response, and swung inwards instinctively. Then, as quickly as he had braked, your man repeated his two fingered gesture and accelerated off madly again. On the spot, our soothing radio was turned off and the air was blue as Eoin cursed and swore and, stepping on the accelerator, determined to show that so and so his tail lights the very minute the oncoming traffic eased just a little. I had no doubt he would too, we having the advantage in horsepower. I, metaphorically tightening my seat belt and pressing the imaginary brakes on the passenger's side, hoped that other driver would continue to speed onwards. However, Eoin's determination and superior horsepower meant that we soon caught up again. We still could not pass out and immediately the other driver spotted us the same antic of suddenly braking, two fingered salutes and instant acceleration was repeated all over again.

So, my discretion overcoming Eoin's valour, we slowed speed, and let some of the cars now behind us, to pass out, to put them and distance between us and that manic driver. But your man now would have none of that. He also slowed to let them all pass him by, and then, dropping his speed suddenly, repeated his performance all over again.

'Will you for God sake pull in and stop a while and let that madman go on about his business,' I implored Eoin, a foolish suggestion, with hindsight, because Eoin would be no match for that young man, physically, if he had decided to stop as well.

Then, however, Eoin had an absolute brainwave. He grabbed the mobile phone, held it up and pretended to be dialling a number, the Gardaí being the obvious choice. The young man, however, repeated his braking manoeuvre, thus seemingly showing his contempt for anything we could do. But the ploy seemingly worked because he then accelerated suddenly, and shot across the road, disappearing down a bye road right in front of a truck. I must admit I shut my eyes tight, certain there would be a horrendous impact. The immediate squeal of the truck's brakes, as the truckdriver burned rubber, saved that young pup's life, and there's nothing surer. Luckily there also was no innocent vehicle behind the truck

We drove on, shocked and somewhat chastened. I wrote

down the car number. But we decided to do nothing about it even though we had the phone in the car, purely for selfish reasons I must admit. We did not want the hassle of making statements, and, apart from the fright we all had got, there was no real harm done. Now if the truck had hit him, or there had been a pile up because of his actions, it would have been a different story entirely. Then I would have taken great vindictive pleasure in telling our story and disclosing the car number.

Anyway, we got where we were going, safely, and in time too. This, I must admit, was only because of something we noticed on the journey, and that is several people passing out white line huggers, on the inside, a thing we always thought was illegal. Even up one hill, where the slow line was clearly marked and designated, a white line hugger, a young girl this time, was passed, on the inside, by no less than five cars, Kavanaghs included. Well, everybody else seemed to be doing it....

But I wasn't happy about this as a general rule of action. If macho young men don't want to be passed on the outside how will they react to being passed on the inside? But then again, if they are not using their mirrors, and, knowing the speed Eoin drives at, we'd be long gone before they could react.

NOVEMBER

Credentials in Calf-rearing (1995)

Did I tell you at all that Lisa has started to do her certificate in farming this autumn? Well, she has the first module, calf rearing, finished now, and she passed with distinction. She is, therefore, the resident expert, or so everybody teases her. She is very good with calves anyway, patient and thorough and that is really all it takes.

So I have taken two full steps back this year and only feed the calves when everybody else is missing. There can't be two bosses on any job and it suits me fine not to be the one out there all the time. Most days I do take a walk around the calf shed to see how things are going, just as I do take regular 'scoves' through the maternity and waiting wards. I pick my times though, not to be too obvious. Young people must learn and they will never learn with the old people watching their every move. Responsibility and experience are the two best teachers of all.

Certificates in anything just put the icing on the cake, the understanding of why things should be as they are. That is what Lisa is really enjoying in her course, that intellectual stimulation, especially about the physiology of animals. I have been feeding and caring for calves for umpteen years but I bet Lisa knows more now than I do about the parts of a calf's stomach, the rumen, reticulum, omasum and abomasum, the oesophageal groove and all that. But she amused me when she told of one piece of advice they were given — if in doubt about the health of a calf, consult someone who knows. And fair dues to her she does just that.

There are only three girls in all doing this farming course. Lisa is not the only married person however. A few of the older men are married as well. But most of the class are young males in their teens. I gather that Lisa is unique in the history of the farming courses generally in being both married and a city girl. Girls doing these courses normally have some rural background. One of her two female companions was also at university with Lisa. Wouldn't the like of girls like those two give you great confidence in the future? And anybody thinking that a farmer's daughter is the only sort of girl desirable as a farmer's wife doesn't know what they are talking about.

Although a little bird told me that single girls who do certificates in farming always have land somewhere there in their background. Taking the courses means that they are then doubly good marriage prospects! I wouldn't know what influence things like that have on a young man going hunting for a wife. I suppose, however, that things haven't changed all that much since my day when we christened one young man at the Macra dances 'How many acres?' He got that nickname when we discovered that he immediately asked every girl with whom he danced, if she was from hereabouts and then inquired as to how many acres there were at home. The third question was about how many brothers and sisters there also were at home. The answers given to all questions determined whether that girl was asked out on the floor by him again or not. He wasn't on for wasting his time. God forgive us but we often put friends up to telling him all sorts of yarns. Still, he did manage to find himself a very nice girl, with no brothers and a fair bit of land to inherit. And they seemingly are living happily ever after with a clutch of children, sons and daughters, one of whom will surely take over after them.

One thing about Lisa going to this class is that it stimulates talk among us all, as to what she did that day. And talk is how the young learn. I often think that parents can be slow to realise that. It isn't enough to show how things are done: it will always be more acceptable if they know why you do it that way as well. Then they can argue with that knowledge, and make a case for trying things a different way, if they can.

With Lisa so full of knowledge these days I had to tell her the story of one of my sons, who, during his first term in Ag.

college, phoned home but didn't want to talk to me. He specifically asked to speak to his Dad. This was a surprise move because the same lad always approached his mother whenever he wanted anything, more money, to be driven somewhere, or whatever. All my sons know quite well who is the soft touch when they lay on the charm. I am the first to admit that. So Eoin went to the phone wondering what on earth could be wrong. He soon found out, however, once the pleasantries were over, Then, that son, in all earnestness, said

'Dad, I don't know how to say this but Mom is rearing the calves all wrong. I wanted to say it last weekend but I couldn't get it out somehow. But I thought if I told you, you might get her straightened out before the cows start calving down again.'

And then he went into a long spiel about how things were being done in the college, the precise quantities of milk per feed, that each new born calf should get only its own dam's beastings, which was to be milked on the spot for freshness, but only fed if the calf didn't suck itself, that a special calf meal was imperative, that I was introducing silage much too early, etc. and etc.

When Eoin came back into the room he was speechless with laughter, and with his long length of a list of my wrong doings in calf rearing which he had jotted down as the conversation progressed. Doubtless it was funny all right. But I was slow enough to see the humour of it. The same fellow, I knew only too well, would give a calf a puck of his fist quicker than a kind word, if it didn't drink on the spot for him.

'Drink it or drown!' I once heard him say as he jammed a calf's head unmercifully into its bucket of milk.

But he wouldn't do that today. His wife wouldn't let him, not even before she passed her module in calf rearing with distinction.

The Tooth Fairy (1996)

When I collected Michaella from school on Friday she came over to me all excitement, and gap-toothed. She is always delighted to see me the odd time I do the school run but this was something extra. Her first tooth was out. It had come out while she was doing her sums and she had it clutched tight in her little fist. And there it stayed all the way home, until I managed to get her to part with it. I only got it away from her by explained the financial consequences to her if she lost it before the tooth fairy came. I also knew there'd be absolute murder with her parents if it was seen to be my fault that her very first tooth was lost by their eldest child.

So, another milestone has been passed this week. But I knew that this particular milestone was fast coming up since I am sure it was with the dint of tugging that that tooth was finally dislodged at school. Michaella has been working hard on it ever since, a week or so ago, during her bath, we had had a long discussion all about how many teeth she had, and which ones would be the first to come out, and the full workings of the tooth fairy.

Michaella loves her bath in my house. But it is no good unless I stay with her. We discuss all sorts of things while she plays with her collection of small empty bottles, the ones I have collected from every and any hotel or guest house I have ever stayed in over the years. I never leave any thing like that after me, even to the extent of each day hiding away anything unused the night before in the expectation that they will be renewed. So, over the years, I have amassed quite a drawer full of the things in my bathroom. There are small soaps, bath oils, shampoos, body lotions, shower caps, shoe polishing cloths, tissues and even sewing kits, all of which I never get around to using.

But I have never taken a towel or anything like that. That would be stealing. But those toiletries are freebies as the Americans would say. In the same way if sweets are given at the end of a meal, even though they are the last thing I want right there and then, there is always room in my handbag for them. Eoin never can understand my compulsion to squirrel anything that is going free. He is even slow to take advantage of the samples given out in the supermarket, saying that he always then feels obliged to buy the product. After my tasting I'll take the product all right from the sales-girl, but I'll also quite happily leave it at the very next place I stop.

For ages those single servings of bath oils and the like have been more or less useless reminders of my magpie tendencies, unless I ran out of something or was having visitors. Since my granddaughters came along, however, the stash is diminishing rapidly. At bath-times Michaella always goes to that drawer for her very own container of bubble bath and shampoo. And all the empty bottles are kept in another drawer because, in the bath, filling them and emptying them keeps her and Nicole happy for ages, better than all the bath toys going.

Their bath time in this house has been known to last well over an hour. We have, after all, a whole routine to go through, both in, and out, of the bath. Recently, without fail, we sing Ten Green Bottles over and over, as Michaella makes sure that the right number of water filled little bottles accidentally fall. Now, on Friday, having discussed how the tooth fairy came in the dark, and would know immediately that the tooth was under the pillow when it saw the gap in Michaella's mouth, we ranged up twenty small bottles on the edge of the bath and together changed the song to new words:

Twenty white teeth in Missy Michaella's mouth,
Twenty white teeth in Missy Michaella's mouth,
And if one white tooth comes accidentally out,
There'll be nineteen white teeth in Missy Michaella's mouth.

And then a bottle cover then was put up on the other side to represent the money she'd get from the tooth fairy as each tooth in her head came out.

It was one complicated business as one lot of numbers went up and the other went down and all had to be celebrated in song. I was losing my way in the sums, but Michaella seemed to have no problem counting both forwards and backwards, something she could not have done six months ago. Her parents think she is very bright, and told me as much lately.

'Is she much brighter than the average five-year-old?' I enquired, tongue firmly in cheek because each and every one of my children boast of their children being taller, brighter, or better in so many ways than the average child of the same age. Was there a parent yet who did not think the same? Yet what has become of all those extraordinarily bright children? Like mine, I dare say they just grew up.

I have great hopes for Missy Michaella, however. I had dis-
suaded her from taking the tooth into the bath with her on
Friday night. But she insisted on playing Twenty White Teeth in
Missy Michaella's Mouth a second time and suggested, win-
ningly, that I should get her pound coins instead of the bottle
caps, to put up on the other side, since, after all, that was what
the tooth fairy was going to bring her.

I compromised, with a pound coin just for the tooth that was
out. This she did not leave in the drawer with the rest of the
stuff, for the next time. Instead, she took it home with her. And
there she told her mother that a pound was the going rate for
the tooth fairy, and not ten pence, because Diyee had said so.
And she also told her mother all about the great new game.

So I had better start collecting pound coins before the next
bath night here, or, better again, teach Michaella the law of
diminishing returns and find out if she really is brighter than
the average six year old, which she will be in just two weeks. I
wonder what will she coax out of me for that occasion?

Did I Go or Was I Pushed? (1998)

I miss farming. There I've said it. That has been a little sore
festering away in the back of my mind for quite some time and
I've never really put words to it before, not even to Eoin. I well
remember, though, once being asked if I had voluntarily given
up my farming work, or was I pushed? I avoided answering the
direct question at the time, which was easy enough since my
questioner really only wanted to tell me her own story of how
she felt that her son and daughter-in-law would be just as
happy never to see her out in the farmyard at all, especially
during the school holidays when her schoolteacher daughter-in-
law is at home full time. And each time she senses a nose in the
air or that little bit of an atmosphere, whether it is real or
imagined, she feels hurt and finds herself then staying away
deliberately and sulking. Now she didn't use the word sulking
of course but I am as well able as the next to read between the
lines since I too have been there and done that!

That moment of self-recognition was soon pushed to the back of my mind. It resurfaced, however, when lying in a hospital bed, all last Thursday afternoon, and most of Friday as well, waiting for another little procedure to be done on my back. Eoin, of course, had me in that hospital miles too early. 'There's no doubt about it Liz — some day you are going to be late for your own funeral,' he had said, crossly, to me earlier that Thursday morning. This was hardly the most tactful of things to say to a woman on her way into hospital but he is ever and always the same. He is positively paranoid about being on time, no matter where we are going.

'I'm sure that half past two isn't really critical,' I assured him for the umpteenth time as I finally threw my few things together. Eoin had urged me to pack my case immediately after breakfast while I, instead, wanted to personally make sure that all my indoor plants were watered, the grass cut, and the vegetables weeded. I had a very full morning's work planned — for everybody. I was, of course, suffering from my usual malaise of trying to get everything overdue done at the last minute. I've always been like that before going on holidays or whatever. This time I knew that I'd only be away until the Saturday, but still that compulsion was there to do things that would normally stay on the long finger for days, if not weeks.

I even started to iron Eoin's shirts in the bed. This can be done quite easily you know. With the ironing board flat on the bed beside me I can iron as well as I ever did. Despite doing just about everything else in the house since I broke my back, Eoin still cannot manage to open the ironing board. It was when finally faced with nothing but badly wrinkled shirts, one day he demanded that I show him how in blazes the thing worked. His fussing and fuming and general air of being hard done by was so bad that I then discovered my ability to iron in the bed. Ironing, in or out of the bed, was never my favourite household chore, however. That was why I still had heaps of ironing left that morning, when the lot, ironed and un-ironed, and the ironing board was forcibly taken from me and I had no choice but to give in, do my packing and come quietly. Yet, despite all my deliberate dawdling, we were still in the hospital miles too early.

So, there I was, tucked into my narrow hospital bed, with

not a thing to do but wait. Eoin left me there do some shopping
down town. He was back, however, almost immediately, to
hand me the new issue of the *Farmers' Journal* which he had
spotted in the hospital shop on his way out. 'There! That will
keep you quiet now until I get back!' was his comment as he
again left. And doubtless it once would have. But now, picking
up a book instead, I had to face the reality that this was no
longer the case. For months back I have actively avoided what I
once devoured. Always it was a bit of an unspoken tussle
between Eoin and myself, who'd get hold of the *Journal* first. We
both wanted it immediately, to find out what was new in farming.

The fact that this is no longer the way for me I never mentioned to Eoin. I am not sure that he has even noticed that I
never once look for the *Journal* and indeed that it can remain un-
opened on my bed for days. I, myself, was not fully aware of all
that, under cover of an interesting television programme or a book
in hands. Even my knitting those winter months served as a blind
to the fact that it hurts me to read of things pertaining to farming when I no longer have hand, act or part in what, for all my
mature years, was the main spring and driving force of my life.

My being placed firmly on the sidelines took place long before
I broke my back, however. That just confirmed it. My broken
back also successfully cloaked the fact of my resentment, even
from myself. My evasive action in not reading about the nitty-
gritty of farming was purely a subconscious self-protective
device. Only now do I understand why a survey some time ago
showed that retired farmers still got the *Journal*, but did not
read it thoroughly any more. Active farmers, of any age or sex,
were the ones who read it from cover to cover.

Anyway, my trip to hospital was not to philosophise about
farm retirement and its effects on the psyche. A long day's
fasting finally led to my visit to the theatre at four o'clock where
long lasting painkillers and steroids were injected into my
spine. Much later that night I found that I could walk more
easily, but with a loss of balance. My body had obviously
adapted to walking one way because of a particular pain and
now has to adapt itself once more, which doubtless it will. The
human body, and mind, is amazing in its power of adaptation,
even if it also cloaks the why and wherefore from our conscious

minds. It's just too bad, however, that since this particular hospital stay, I no longer can keep up the pretence to myself, whatever about to everybody else, that I heroically retired of my own accord in order to give the young people room.

The Prodigal Son (1997)

I had better be careful today and not repeat the old mistake of parents making such a great fuss of the son or daughter, whom they only see occasionally, that the family at home feel justly aggrieved. I must keep well in mind the tale of the Prodigal Son, for whom the father killed the fatted calf, to the great resentment of his stay-at-home brother. I can nearly hear that poor, hardworking, lad muttering to himself — 'and after all I've done for them...'

Well, we didn't quite kill the fatted calf for Seamus last weekend, but we came pretty close to it. 'He'll be mad for a good feed of rashers and eggs anyway' said Eoin, as he made out his shopping list in advance, remembering just how awful the bacon was during our one trip to the States. I had to smile to myself when I saw the load of food that Eoin then brought back for our son's short visit, knowing that there was no way we'd get to eat even the half of it in just two days, even though things like the smoked salmon would hold fine. And, he had also booked a table at our nearest restaurant, which is only at the bottom of our hill, for the Saturday night — so that was one night out of the reckoning as well. Now I am not getting at Eoin in this because that is exactly the way I too have always behaved when family members are arriving. I'm even worse when their wives are coming with them. Then I find myself indulging in a frenzy of house cleaning as well, with the usual result that I'm exhausted and not at my best when they arrive.

To be quite honest, however, it's lovely though, to get a son all by himself for a bit, without any appendages. Then they seem to slip more easily back into their old roles and are much more giving of themselves. The presence of a partner changes them, and us, in a number of subtle ways. I know my own mother too really enjoyed best when any of us visited her on our own, for a really long chat. There'd be nothing said really that could not be said in the presence of our spouses, children, and in the last few years, my grandchildren. She loved to see those too, but occasionally only. Really it was her own children she needed to come and visit her. I know other mothers feel exactly the same way as well. It is actually a sour enough joke with one of my friends because she and her husband take little bets between themselves on how long one particular son will be in their house before the phone will go and he'll be called away. His wife invariably needs him, urgently, sometimes in five minutes, but never more than half an hour. And he always goes on the spot, mobile phone in hand.

Of course if we had such things in my day perhaps I'd have been just as bad as that daughter-in-law. Eoin, from the very first day we came home from our honeymoon, never missed a day without going to see his mother, who lived, without a telephone, in a bungalow on the land. I remember, our very first Christmas Eve together here, for one reason or another, Eoin hadn't managed to see her all that day and he set off after supper to visit her even though she was coming here to us the next day for Christmas dinner. I was more than annoyed because Christmas Eve was the big thing to me at that stage, finishing up the decorations, lighting the candle, wrapping presents, and all that sort of stuff. Now I know that I was as jealous as hell that Eoin was putting his mother before my wishes and probably made that very clear to him — for all the good it did me. Eoin, while his mother lived, never missed a day without going to see her, even though I mightn't always be told.

There is no way that I could say the same thing about any of my lot today. But then I gave no thought at all to how my own mother might have been feeling that very first Christmas Eve with me, the first of her brood gone — and it was, after all, from her that I got my own feelings about Christmas Eve being special. Eoin and I went up next day all right to deliver our presents. So, perhaps, I am now only reaping what I sowed? We won't go into that, however, it's too painful a subject. This past weekend with Seamus was glorious. I both ate and drank too much, and I laughed a lot at his tales of his youth and smiled secretly to myself when he told of some of the problems he is now having with his teenage children. Human nature doesn't change and history does keep repeating itself, no matter how much any individual may try to change it.

Things may not always be as they seem on the surface, however, and we should be aware of that. As something of a cautionary tale I told Seamus of my friend whose son always gets called away in no time flat, by his wife, when he comes to visit his mother.

'But hasn't it ever occurred to you, or her, that maybe that son of hers has it all arranged beforehand, with his wife, to phone and rescue him within a set time...?' said Seamus in reply. Ouch!

Assertive or Aggressive? (1998)

'Well ... and how's my aggressive woman this morning?' said Eoin to me as he brought me my breakfast tray. Now there was a Freudian slip if ever I heard one: he could only have been thinking about the assertiveness course I had started the night before.

My family, when they first heard of my latest notion, thought it the funniest thing ever. 'That, surely, is the very last thing that Mom needs,' said one son to his father. I could have retorted how little he really knows. But that would only serve to open up a whole new can of worms. In actual fact, I decided to attend this assertiveness course, firstly, because it is on in the parish and so I can get there easily, and secondly, to satisfy my curiosity as to what assertiveness courses are all about. Now, after only a couple of sessions, I realise that really I'm going because I genuinely need just such a course to set me straight on a lot of things.

Eoin drives me there, and, having wheeled me into place, goes off home until it is time to collect me once more. He also thinks that I'm slightly mad but humours me as one would a sick child. On collecting me, he, of course, wants to know what went on for the past two hours. But, after I tell him, as much as I can, I often think he is no wiser than when I started. One really has to be there to understand. The best way I can explain it is to say that one embarks on a voyage of self-discovery and I, for one, am not yet quite sure where I am going to finish up.

I am having to rethink quite a few things about my life. It is easy enough for me to be assertive. But it is hard indeed for me to then deal with the results of my assertiveness. Women, mothers especially, have to walk an extremely thin line between assertiveness and aggressiveness. Men have it much easier. They are taught, from a very early age, to stand up for themselves, to be their own person.

Actually, people are conditioned, by our very language, to dislike the term assertive in connection with women. Dominant, controlling, commanding, imperious, authoritative and aggressive are the words my in-built computer thesaurus threw up when I asked it for alternative meanings for the word assertive. Now, put any of those words before 'man' and they don't sound half as bad as when put before 'woman', now do they? But, when my machine then told me that humble, obscure, reserved, modest, secondary and subordinate were the antonyms or opposites of assertive I got quite a shock of recognition. Those are just the attributes that the good nuns, and others, tried to develop in me during my formative years. The fact that they failed, spectacularly, is neither here nor there. The residue remains. As I said it is easy enough being assertive. But it is hard indeed to walk away feeling good about it afterwards, no matter how right one is.

So, when we all got a sheet of paper detailing individual rights of everybody, no matter who, this was a revelation to me. My conditioning has always been that other people had rights in life whereas I had duties. The young girls, at the course, couldn't quite grasp this fact, I think, even though I was not alone in this way of thinking. I am learning just as much from my companions as I am from the course material — I had not realised just how much I was missing mental stimulation from others during my long convalescence.

Out of the listed twelve rights on our sheet of paper we each had to say which jumped out at us, as most relevant to our own personal situation. Now I am only going to talk for myself, everything anybody else on this assertiveness course says, is, naturally enough, totally confidential. We are all revealing of our inner selves in our answers, our body language, etc. even more than we realise perhaps. This course is designed to help us understand ourselves, and our rights, as well as the games people play, be it consciously or unconsciously.

Now a lot of the rights on our lists bore no relevance for me. I know I have the right to say yes or no for myself just as I have the right to ask for more information when I don't fully understand something. Yet I do know that many people will not, for instance, ask their doctor for more detail, ever. And, dealing with teachers seems to be a major problem for too many young mothers. But what jumped out at me personally, was number three on the list. I have the right to express my values and opinions without having to justify them. Now there's a thought. Most of the rows here are because I feel obliged to justify my values and opinions to my family, be they sons or daughters-in-law. That's when I have been told, more than once, that there is no need at all for me to get so aggressive. In future I shall just say what I think, straight out, and then walk away without even trying to justify myself. Then there cannot be any cross words spoken for the simple reason that I'll be long gone....

The only thing wrong with that perfect scenario is one unfortunate little fact. Having said my say, I am physically unable to walk away from anybody, whatever about being able to do so mentally...? And, in that respect, not even this assertiveness course has succeeded in making me strategically deaf. Still and all, we have several nights yet to go before the Christmas break. And I intend to get in some practice in the meantime.

Great Expectations (1998)

Most established writers talk of how much they hate and detest the chore of attending book signings. But I'd be a liar if I didn't admit that, while it lasted, I was very flattered each time I was asked to do a signing. I also accepted all invitations since I cannot in truth claim that I was engulfed by requests for my presence after *Home to Roost* was published.

The first signings were great in every sense. I loved meeting the people and was gratified when small queues formed waiting to talk to me. But they all were very soon after my performance on the *Late Late Show* and no more signings are booked until one the Sunday before Christmas. So, in this pre-Christmas lull, I was delighted to be asked to do another at short notice. Full of confidence, I set off for the shopping centre at the appointed time. I had my good pen in my pocket and Eoin had brought three more biros lest my refill ran out.

I duly arrived, all smiles. There was nobody there, however, except the two owners of the book shop. My smile weakened little by little as we all made small talk, vacuous chit-chat which was only interrupted when, occasionally, both of them had to attend to customers, buying books other than mine. I managed to send Eoin off to the section to do with horses, while I pretended to be engrossed by the books on accountancy near where my wheelchair was parked. I'd see him looking worriedly at me occasionally so I'd smile bravely back, assuming a nonchalance I was far from feeling, and signalling him to stay where he was. I even got to wishing that the owners would not feel so obliged to keep coming back to me with offers of cups of coffee or tea, all of which I refused feeling that these would make my solitary state still more conspicuous.

Finally, a young woman approached me. I grasped her hand like a drowning woman when she said how she had enjoyed me on the *Late Late*. All my pent-up emotions went into entertaining her feverishly even though she had brought no copy of *Home to Roost* for me to sign. Eventually the poor woman said she must get a copy of my book, which fortunately were close to hand. So she had no means of escape and I signed her copy for which she perforce then had to pay. I beamed at her as she left: at least the night wasn't a total disaster.

Another *Late Late* viewer then came with my book in hand, which she was buying as a Christmas present for her mother even though neither she, nor her mother, had anything to do with farming. Thank God for the *Late Late* and Gay Byrne, I thought, on her departure, and may the Lord send me some more of his admirers, quickly. It was not to be, however. My third, and final, customer was a young man. He said he had grown up reading Liz on the *Farmers' Journal* and he just wanted to put a face to the name. He hadn't come specially to buy my book or anything like that. He was just passing and saw the sign.

I didn't care what he was doing just as long as he stopped a while, and bought a book. So I heard all about how he chose engineering as a career but his brother was still on the home place. That was how he still read the *Journal* from time to time. Being of the same age as my sons, he had related very much to them when growing up, he said, and that by my writing about their escapades, his own misdemeanours had seemed minor in comparison. He, for example, had dented the front of his parents' car the same week as one of my sons had totally written off our car, and finished up in hospital to boot. So I had done him a great favour, with his parents, when they read my article that week, he told me.

After this young man made his escape I sat in solitary state for the best part of another hour before I, in turn, felt free to make good my own escape. But my hosts insisted that I stay just a little longer. I could hardly demur in the face of my failure to generate any extra business for them. I felt far worse for their predicament than I did for my own. My feelings of guilt were vastly inflated, however, when I found I had only been delayed while one of them went to collect a magnificent bouquet of flowers for me. My visit had cost them much more than I had made for them in sales. And, far from slinking quietly away when my time was up, my tail between my legs, all eyes were on me as I left, my arms full of florist flowers, and the books on horse racing Eoin said he just felt compelled to buy.

DECEMBER

Things Must Be Just Right... (1998)

'I must have ten juniper berries,' said Eoin plaintively as he went through the store cupboard for the ingredients to marinate the venison he had just bought. He had that in one hand and his recipe under his chin while he rooted around with the other hand for peppercorns, wine vinegar and virgin olive oil. A choice of bowls stood on the bench and it was panic stations all round as he gathered his ingredients together for his last night's cookery class.

Things falling, and his swearing, brought me out to investigate even though this was the sort of pre-cookery-class commotion I've grown accustomed to these past six weeks. And, between this, and his first six weeks last Spring, the press I call my store cupboard, is now dangerously full of jars of all kinds of condiments, and stuff such as I never dreamed of having. Anchovies and sun-dried tomatoes never figured in my class of cooking and that's for sure. As for juniper berries, I had never even seen the things, not to mind used them. The assistants at the two supermarkets had also looked blankly at Eoin when he asked them if they stocked them. He had found it hard enough to find his kilo of venison. So, as you can gather, this is no basic cookery class for helpless men that my man is attending.

Each week the class is given a couple of pages of recipes to pick the one they like best. And Ally, their teacher, demonstrates a dish for them, as well. So there is a lot going on with Ally and her fifteen pupils all doing different dishes. There is a lot going on as well besides the cooking. I think Eoin enjoys the

camaraderie every bit as much as the cooking: he comes home
with a fund of stories as well as his cooked dish each week.
There are just the two men there this time, Eoin and his friend
Harold. And four of the girls who did the course with them last
time are pregnant this time, including their teacher. This has
absolutely nothing to do with the two bucks, of course, except,
perhaps, in their dreams. The timing is wrong for one thing.
And, as we all know, timing is everything.

Eoin is, at last, getting his timing perfect, in cooking dinner.
His big trouble always was in synchronising dishes. He could
never get everything ready at one and the same time. His meat
dish would be ready while his potatoes were still rock hard in
the middle. And it took him a long time to realise that some
vegetables take a lot longer to cook than others and never ever
take as long as meat in a stew. For ages it was a complete mystery to him just where his vegetables had disappeared to when
he could find no trace of his carefully chopped efforts in the
finished product.

Chopping was another problem. As well as all that stuff for
the store cupboard Eoin bought himself a whole new set of
really good kitchen knives. These were so sharp that he regularly sliced through a bit of a finger as well. He still has a box of
plasters in the kitchen for emergency use because I notice that,
now he is in charge, those knives are jealously guarded. There is
no longer the quick borrowing of a sharp knife to deal with an
emergency outside. I was nearly killed when I once took one of
them to do a little trimming back of one of my house plants.
Ever since those knives are kept up high, he says to keep them
safe from the small girls. I strongly suspect, however, it is the
old girl he really has in mind. But never mind. I'm not complaining. I think I was never so well fed in my life.

To get back to the venison and juniper berries, however, that
is possibly where men and women differ so much in this cooking lark. Eoin has to have absolutely everything right before he
starts. Indeed, getting ready is a major operation. Everything is
laid out, ready to go, with much checking back on the list of
necessary ingredients. And everything is also weighed most
accurately. There is none of a pinch of this, a shake of that and a
guess at the weight of a lump of meat or a quantity of flour. I

even saw the eggs for a sponge cake being weighed to ensure that each was the exact two ounces. That time it took part of an extra egg to make the proportions exactly right. The rest of that egg was growing mould when I found it in the fridge and threw it out.

There was no fear of his venison growing mould, however, soaking as it was for a full twenty-four hours, precisely, in loads of red wine, spices, etc. The marinade also had an extra ingredient to overcome the lack of juniper berries. I suddenly remembered that juniper is used to flavour gin. So the venison got a real good slosh from the gin bottle and Eoin was happy his list of ingredients was complete. The venison smelt gorgeous when Eoin came home last night. He was a little sad that the course was over, however. But most of the gang have agreed to be back again when Ally gives her next class.

'With foal at foot by then I presume?' said the bold Harold, as they all regretfully packed up for the moment. I'm betting, however, that they'll all be back for the next session, however, regardless of what's afoot.

Where Has All the Magic Gone? (1977)

If I were to start an 'I hate Christmas' society how many of you would join? If truth were told I'd say I would have to close the membership list very early on, because these days I fear that Christmas only seems to be really enjoyed by small children and those enjoying the anticipation of going home for the Christmas. The parents, in each case, also enjoy it, but to a much lesser degree.

For the rest of us, it is the anticlimax of the year. We spend simply ages building up to it now that the first faint signs of Christmas begin in October. By mid November it is in full swing with cards and candles, tinsel and toys, cakes and carols. Not that there is anything wrong with all of that. It does add a certain excitement to the streets and the chore of shopping is at least more colourful with all the Christmas packaging.

I now look with pleasure at all the tots going to see Santa —

but pity greatly the poor harassed parents. Thank God my time
for carting my youngsters through the crowds for that, is well
and truly over. We, then, inevitably finished up with at least one
of the sons crying, another in a black sulk, more of them disappointed, all fighting, and, on one notable occasion, one lost
with the Gardaí notified of same. Before the outing was over,
Eoin and I, would usually be spoiling for a fight too and mad
anxious to get out of the chaos of the city and home as soon as
humanly possible.

All that fuss and excitement peaked with me anyway on
Christmas Eve — always the best day of the whole season as far
as I was concerned. I have always loved the hustle and bustle of
that day, putting the final touches to the Christmas tree; getting
the last piece of holly and ivy out from under our feet; the
turkey bloated with stuffing all ready and waiting for the morrow;
the furtive wrapping and hiding of presents. It was all glorious
anticipation and waiting — and for what?

Christmas Day is just another day, but with much more hard
work than usual. The animals must be looked after, just as on
any other day. All must be fed and the cows must still be
milked, morning and evening. They must still be all bedded and
the yards and cubicles scraped clean of slurry. Work is just the
same as any other day except, because it is Christmas, there is
no help with it. The workmen always have the day completely
off, so the only help Eoin will have will be that, grudgingly
given by sons, dragged away from their television and their
presents. As for me, I'll be cooking, cleaning and refereeing
fights, same as always, only more so. For both farmers and
mothers Christmas certainly is no holiday.

What is wrong, of course, is that now we all have much too
much of everything. It is the old story of every day of the week
being Christmas Day now. There is nothing like a little fast and
abstinence for sharpening any of our little pleasures in life.
Instant gratification in all things has been the ruination of us.
We are now so well fed, every day of the week, that it is well
nigh impossible to provide real novelties for the family on
Christmas Day. Turkey is no longer a once-a-year treat. We had
one here for the boys home from school at Halloween, and for
Pádraig's birthday in August. So it is no novelty for Christmas.

Fruit and vegetables of all kinds are also available to us all the year round, either fresh or out of the freezer. Last year my brood requested rice pudding and tinned pears for their Christmas Day dessert. They were 'sick of cake, raspberries, strawberries and all that sort of stuff,' they informed me.

There was a lot to be said for the Christmas Eve of my childhood with its salty stock-fish for putting an edge to our appetite for goose and its trimmings the next day. Another great appetite sharpener was the very early double Mass on Christmas Day itself. This is now, also a thing of the past. I well remember being forcibly taken from my bed before dawn when I had just gone back to sleep after seeing what Santa had left at the end of my bed. It was such an unreal feeling then, in the near pitch dark, travelling to Mass in the pony and trap, my hand-knitted red pixie on my head to keep my ears warm. All that was a special part of Christmas. The stars then seemed to be so bright and near and the luminosity of the dawn sky made me want to reach out and grab great fists of it to keep the moment fixed for ever. The tiredness, the excitement, and the strangeness of it all combined to form a tight knot in my stomach.

I can still smell the hot-house chrysanthemums on the altar and see the altar-boys in their red soutanes and white surplices, like me, all glassy-eyed with exhaustion. I can even hear the exultant singing of the *Adeste Fideles* breaking the stillness. The Latin added so much to the magic and the mystery. But the seemingly unending second Mass, which started immediately the first Mass was over, was really too much for children when the cold and excitement made their need for the toilet imperative. The shaming warm trickle down one's legs was something I tried to keep hidden.

Of such were my personal Christmas morning memories. Eoin, who lived outside Rathdrum, Co. Wicklow, at that stage of his childhood, most remembers stepping out into the pre-dawn dark and seeing the whole mountainside like a gigantic Christmas tree, with the whole parish, men, women and children, making their way down to the church for the six o'clock Mass and each carrying a storm lantern to guide their way down the mountain paths. He says that the soft, warm, yellow lights twinkled and flashed in their hundreds, appeared and disappeared from sight, weaving intricate patterns as they were carried along winding pathways. Gradually then the lights lessened at the top of this tapestry and gathered and thickened as the people met on the valley road, to form a veritable river of light. There was no rural electrification, on even hope of it in the mountains of Wicklow then. The moon was the only parish lamp.

I can just imagine the meeting and greeting that then went on with all the neighbours walking to Mass there during those war years when all the cars were off the road and bicycles and ponies were impractical due to the steepness of the mountain paths and the frequency of ice and snow. Eoin says that I was spoilt rotten tucked under the rugs in our pony and trap while he, and all his family, walked briskly to get warm. Be that as it may, for both of us, once we were home from Mass, the rest of Christmas Day stretched on endlessly, with all the time in the world to read and play and eat, with no thought to mother hard at it in the kitchen or father outside with work to be done.

How history repeats itself?

Continuity Counts (1994)

I had my granddaughters here for the day today because their parents were gone to town to bring home the Christmas: if they didn't they said there would be nothing left in the shops. Michaella is now of an age, almost four, when she is into everything and as cute as a pet fox. So, far away from all activity was the safest place for her to be, lest she see too much. Her birthday, being near Christmas, means that occasion must also be covered in advance. So Missy has the job at the moment of deciding what Santa is bringing her, and what she wants to get for her birthday. I asked her both questions today and she told me that she wanted some special doll, 'Dolly All Gone', it sounded like.

'Maybe Santa will bring you that?' I queried, afraid of duplication. But she was adamant that he wouldn't because Daddy had told her that Santa was bringing her quite enough.

'He has to bring things to everybody else too, Diyee, all over the world. So I can't get Dolly All Gone, never, ever,' she said to me as sorrowful as an old woman.

Then she put her head on one side and said, as coaxingly as could be: 'Will you buy me Dolly All Gone, Diyee?'

And, seeing a chink of hope with the smile on my face, she was then up on my lap, hugging the life out of me and planting kiss after kiss firmly on my lips. So what else could I do but say that if I could find one I'd buy it for her birthday. She then, however, was able to tell me precisely the shop she saw it in, and that it was up high, but I was big enough all right to get it down.

Eoin says that I totally spoil Michaella and jump to her every whim. But how can I resist when she puts her arms about me and tells me that I am her bestest friend and she loves me to bits. And these kisses and hugs come often without obvious reason. Those are the ones that melt me totally. Of course the times when I produce something for her I expect her delight. And at those times I often think of my mother.

She kept a constant supply of goodies for all visiting children. She always said that it is a case of cupboard love with children, they are all fond of those who give them 'something nice'. And true enough, every time we visited Mamma, Michaella went straight to the plank of sweets and crisps. Now there is a word that my mother used. To plank a thing is to hide it, or a plank is a place where things are hidden. Goodness knows where the word comes from, but Mamma had lots of words from her own childhood that we used as a matter of course. A hen to us was never cackling, it was craking. Sometimes to this day my sons ask me precisely what a word I use means and then I realise it is one of my mother's.

How could my sons understand however, when many of my mother's words were of farming practices that are now no more? Hens no longer crake in the farmyards and wynds of hay no longer stand in the fields. A wynd was a cock of hay so big that a person, usually someone young, stood up on it all the time it was being made, receiving the pikes of hay from several more family members piking it up. And it was always piking hay never forking it. Many is the wynd or cock like that that I stood on in my youth and the only ease then was while the tumbling paddy, a kind of a horse drawn hay rake, gathered in a few more swaths together, and the base was made for the next wynd. While this was going on one could lie down for a little while and watch the white clouds scurrying by in the blue, blue sky, while dreaming teenage dreams.

There was a definite place for family labour in those years, especially in our case, since my father died when we were still young. I often told the boys here, when they were reluctant to return to school, that my brother and I used always say that we were going back to our boarding schools, in September, 'for our holidays'. But we never gave a thought to our mother and how she felt on those long, lonely, winter, months of her early widowhood. She often later did tell me that it was the sheer volume of work that kept her sane and going. There isn't time to wallow in grief, she held, when one is really and truly physically exhausted. And we, as teenagers, never got into the slightest trouble either because there just was no time or energy left for anything like that.

Thinking of Michaella's birthday reminds me of my mother as she died just three days after Michaella's birthday last year. And, as well, when giving Missy her bath tonight, she suddenly noticed my wedding ring and asked why I had two rings. I told her that the day her great-grandmother had died I, as the eldest daughter, had put on her wedding ring to wear in memory of her. Michaella thought about that for a while, looking up at me with the pink cheeks and perfect skin of babyhood, and then she said, quite matter of factly, having worked the whole thing out for herself:

'You had no little girls, Diyee, only boys, so will you give me your ring the day you die? My hand will be all big then!'

She then slipped off my rings to see how they would fit on her little fingers. I pointed out the names and dates inscribed inside the two rings and explained what they meant. All this meant nothing to an almost four-year-old of course, but it did to me.

Continuity counts.

Christmas Card Players (1977)

It has started already, the Christmas popularity contest, and we've still two weeks to go. Although some of the players have dropped out, many women still enter the popularity stakes and vie with others as to the most effective way to display their trophies. Younger women seem to be the most vulnerable, especially in those first unsure years of marriage. I, too, once played that game, and with some success.

When I found it was costing me quite a lot of money, however, to climb that particular social ladder, I gave up sending Christmas cards to all and sundry. Instead I write to far-away relatives and friends, the ones we are not likely to see in the near future. Eoin of course, like most Irish men, lets his side of the family totally to me. I know it is more trouble to sit down and write a proper letter, but the replies make it worthwhile. It is much more satisfactory to hear how life is treating them all, what stage Johnny is at or how Mary did in her exams, than just to get a picture of a robin in the snow and a message 'With best wishes from all the Murphy's'. We can surely take their good wishes towards us for granted any day of the week. Friends or relations who can't be bothered writing to us in return can send still us a card if they like. But they'll get no return trophy from me anymore, to grace their mantelpiece or wherever. I am happy that all the old aunts and far-away friends much prefer a chatty letter to a card with its sentimental verse and my hastily scribbled signature.

To come back to the games people play, however, it is easy to spot the really-in-earnest Christmas card players. Theirs will be the very first card to drop into your letter-box. It comes early, to act as a reminder not to forget them with your return card. Having their card on Christmas Eve wouldn't be much good now would it? while it might elicit a New Year card the most likely effect would be only to ensure them being on next year's list.

Getting the cards is only part of the story, however, The display is the thing. After all, what use is it in getting the world and all of cards if as many people as possible don't see them, and be suitably amazed and impressed. Last Friday, after the Country Market, I dropped back some of her unsold stuff to a neighbour. Having refused an offer of coffee I was still taken into her front room to see her Christmas decorations. But it was really to see her cards that I was invited in. There they were, all those cards, marching in serried ranks, over the mantelpiece, across the piano top, dropping onto the occasional tables. but more significantly, barely speckling the many strips of red crêpe paper hanging down all four walls.

'Sure there are still over two weeks left to Christmas,' she explained, no doubt following the direction of my eyes. 'After all, I got 196 Christmas cards last year.'

I was suitably impressed and made all the right noises as I examined her hoard as was expected of me. There, however, I saw the names of some of her near neighbours and also many of those she had seen at the Country market that very morning and will see again there for the next two Fridays. It would make you wonder wouldn't it.

Then, last night, we went to a fork-supper at a friend's house, the very first of our Christmas dos. Clare (not her real name) had all her decorations up and had criss-crossed her living room with twine and tinsel and then slung her cards all along those. That was fine for Clare and Bill (also not his real name), who are of barely average height. Eoin, however, is quite a tall man and he bumped into the strings a few times, at their lowest points, and knocked some cards to the ground.

At home, he later imparted a most interesting little bit of information as we got ready for bed. When he had picked up the cards, after his first collision, he noticed that one of them was from an ex-girlfriend of his and he commented to himself that she was still using green ink. Later on he noticed the same green ink, on another card, and out of sheer curiosity looked at the writing, to find it was from the same person. So, the question exercising his mind for the rest of the evening was whether his old girlfriend was getting forgetful and had sent Clare two Christmas cards this year, or whether Clare had bulked our her cards for her party by using those she had kept over since last year.

Which would you think is the correct answer?

A Christmas Robin (1998)

This is to be a very special Christmas. Once more there is a baby here just in time. It's funny how things turn out. Last year we were full of sorrow for hopes dashed. Now, almost twelve months later to the day, we had a very special delivery early last week, a Christmas Robyn.

Yes, we've got a new granddaughter, all ten pounds eleven and a half ounces of her, and she is absolutely perfect. Her father is floating high on a cloud of delight and her mother, although sore, is quite well after a Caesarean section. I wonder does she fully realise quite how fortunate she was not having to deliver a first baby of that size?

Mother and child are both home now, as is Eoin Óg. He has practically lived in the hospital since the birth. It is a good job he had changed to spring calving otherwise something would have got to give. I have never seen such a doting father before. His happiness catches at my heart. As my mother would say, 'He's so very happy — sure God love him' — an expression of hers I never fully understood before although everybody else did when they heard her use those exact same words on the day of my wedding.

But that was a long time ago. Still, my mother is very much in my thoughts this week, the fifth anniversary of her death. Births have a funny way of making us older people think of the generations past, anyway, as we look for resemblance's in the newcomer. Not that one should always say what one sees of course. I once told a neighbour that his son took after the mother's side and the proud father was highly offended. He said that anybody with half an eye in their head could see that his son was the spitting image of the O'Sullivans, seed, breed and generation of them. And he wasn't, then or now. I have never seen a young man quite so like his mother in every way.

Still, ever since, as a rule of thumb I always say that baby boys take after the father's side and that baby girls are the image of their mother's, regardless. This time, however, it seems to be quite true. Robyn strongly resembles her maternal grand-mother, and thus her mother as well since they are very alike and growing more so every day that passes. In the hospital, when I looked at all three generations of women together, I was greatly struck by the resemblance.

What really took my fancy, however, was the delight of Lisa's Dad. This was second only to Eoin's Óg's. Of course they are both first-timers since Lisa is an only child, so this is his first grandchild. We are well into double figures on grandchildren now. Still, we got in as soon as we could after the birth, for that all important bonding process. Then, when the other grandparents came in, for their second visit, I was in undisputed possession of Robyn and found myself really loth to hand her over to her other grandmother. But once I did, I found myself enveloped in a great bear hug by her other grandfather and, only for the condition I'm in, I'd say that I'd have been danced all over the ward as we both agreed that at last we had seen the day with a grandchild in common between us.

I was also thoroughly kissed on the strength of that, very nice too, but once again my mother's words came to my mind. Why does the sight of such really great happiness bring one so close to tears? It wasn't just me you know. Out in the corridor, with Eoin Óg wheeling me along in my chair, I met this other mother who said that she never saw anything like my son when his baby was born. It appears that, after the event, he came tearing out along the corridor, sterile cap and gown still on after the operation, telling everyone, 'It's a girl, it's a girl!' This woman personally thought it was so lovely that a young doctor could still be so very excited about the birth of a baby and said as much to him.

'But it's my daughter — and she's just beautiful,' he exclaimed as he rushed on, the gown flapping behind him. It was only later this woman heard the full story from one of the nurses and, she said, even the nurse was crying a little as she told her. When she herself was gone I heard her full story. Her teenage daughter had just had a baby and she, the mother, was the one at the birth, the father of the baby being long gone. So it was no wonder she was shedding a few tears at what could have been. Even the nurses, who see much too much in this public hospital of absentee fathers and very young mothers, were touched by the delight of all in the birth of this long-awaited child in our family.

I know I've only hinted earlier on at this expected increase in our grandchildren — I was warned off when first we were told the news. And, for once in my life, I was good. After all their problems the young pair worried every step of the way. Now they look set to have the happiest Christmas of their lives, a real family at last — sure God love them.

Happy Christmas everybody.

The Night After Christmas — When It All Began... (1998)

Eoin and I are celebrating an anniversary this Saint Stephen's Day — it is forty-four years now since he first clapped eyes on me, and I on him. I still tease him that he was mildly intoxicated at the time. Otherwise he would never have done as he did that night. Also, my first conscious memory of him is of him leaning against a wall, half-filled glass in hand, keeping time with it to the music.

It was at a Hunt Ball in the era of patent leather dancing shoes, white linen dress shirts with detachable collars which were always sent to the laundry to come back with edges like knife points. Cuff links were essential and most men also had their own, or borrowed, fancy gold or gold-plated button studs glittering down their stiff shirt fronts.

Eoin cut quite a dash. But I had come with another, which was a story in itself. My boyfriend of the time was not available to take me out that night, the really big night of the year, as far as young people and dancing went. You see, there was a total bar on dancing then, throughout all of Advent, as well as Lent. Christmas Day nobody, but nobody, left the sanctity of their own home. So you could say we were frantic for a bit of a dance, and company, come Saint Stephen's Night.

There was nothing facing me, that night, forty four years ago, however, but another night at home. My boyfriend's sister was having an engagement party to which I was not invited. Resigned to my lonesome fate I went to Mass that morning. Yes, most of the parish, young and old, did attend Mass on Stephen's day as well as Christmas day then. Indeed, going to church was often the only social occasion of the week. More happened, both before and after Mass, than the officiating priest was ever made aware.

Coming out of the church that fateful morning, a neighbour, whose sister was a great friend of mine, came up to me and asked would I go to the Hunt Ball with him that night. With not even the slightest hesitation I said yes, miffed as I was with my boyfriend, even though I had never once harboured even the remotest romantic fancy about my proposed escort for the night. Anything would be better than staying in for the night, alone in the bosom of my family. I also had the suitable dress and all the accoutrements. So, after hours spent getting ready, I set off with my escort and it was on with the Ball. All went as predicted, a few dances with neighbours but most with my escort, with whom I also ate supper. Then the unexpected happened. This tall man, to whom I had never spoken in my young life, cut in, and I found myself being whirled onto the floor in the strong arms of Eoin. Having always a liking for tall men I had no objection: my escort that night was barely my own height after all.

Actually, now I look back with wry amusement at my young self. The doorway into my digs in Cork has a terrazzo surround in which I had surreptitiously marked a six-foot point. Then, after a date or two, I'd manoeuvre potential suitors against that wall to see if they measured up. If not, with one brief exception, they were gone. Crazy wasn't it? But, to get back to the night of the Ball, I danced the rest of the night with Eoin, including, unwittingly, the last dance of the night. Not to have that with the person one came with was the unforgivable social faux pas in those times. So, maybe, that was why there wasn't even an attempt at a goodnight kiss when I was left back on my own doorstep once more? One was always walked from the car to the door those times even though there could never be a question of being invited in for a coffee or indeed anything else either.

Once all was over, therefore, I thought no more about the night, knowing I was returning to my normal student life once the holidays were over. However, two days later an old family friend called somewhat unexpectedly. My mother entertained her in the drawing room, the fire being still lit every day for the Christmas, and, when I brought them tea she asked what was all this about my conquest on Stephen's night? I looked at them blankly. But it later transpired that Daisy had come to warn my mother of Eoin's serious intentions, which it appeared he had spoken of widely and loudly, before he and his party had left the bar that night. My escort and I didn't drink at the time so we were probably both tucked up safely in our respective beds by then. Obviously the news spread like wildfire, reaching my mother's ears so quickly. But I only laughed at her mild concern.

Six months later, at Mass, the feast-day of St Peter's and Paul, then a Holiday of Obligation, I was again approached to go to a dance that night. And again I accepted — a summer job keeping me and the same boyfriend apart this time. Now the rest, as they say, is history. You see it was Eoin who accosted me, over the holy water font, going into Mass, this time. And Eoin later told me that he was down at the church gate, twenty minutes early, filling in the time talking to the men standing there, so that he could just casually fall into step with me as I passed though the gate. It took him all the way into the church door to pluck up his courage sufficiently, however, to actually ask me, at the very last moment. and he was so happy when I said yes that he nearly threw his arms around old Paddy Sullivan doing the usual collection in the church porch.

So, all my happy New Years really started, outside our parish church, that Saint Stephen's Day, blossomed over the holy water font the following Saint Peter's and Paul's, and came to fruition inside the same church, on my wedding day, the following October twelve-months.

Happy New Year to everybody.

ALSO FROM LIZ KAVANAGH

COUNTRY LIVING

From May Day nettle soup to mobile phones, from Eoin's PST (pre-silage tension) to the proper colour for wellies, from tussles with the Government to the trials and tribulations of bringing up five great boys — this is Liz Kavanagh at the top of her form! It's all here: the wry humour, the sly descriptions of local characters, the childhood memories, the joys and disasters of life on a farm — all described with Liz Kavanagh's unique blend of wit and homespun wisdom.

ISBN 0-86327-609-1

HOME TO ROOST

On the eve of the publication of *Country Living*, Liz Kavanagh found herself in a hospital bed, with a broken back. The months she spent recovering provided her with much time to reflect on past years and to bring together more of her good-humoured and down-to-earth accounts of the highs and lows of rural life. *Home to Roost* features a cast of characters familiar to Liz's readers everywhere. And there's a surprise visitor here too, dropping in to add her tuppence ha'pence worth....

ISBN 0-86327-686-5

Wolfhound Press
68 Mountjoy Square
Dublin 1